Common-Sense
Classroom Management

**for Special Education Teachers
Grades 6–12**

*This book is dedicated to the many
talented and caring special education teachers
with whom I have worked and to the children they serve.*

Jill Lindberg

*This book is dedicated to my friends and colleagues working in the
field of special education. Over the years, I have had the great fortune
to work with the best of the best—from beginning special educators
to coteachers, supervisors, and college professors. I have
learned so much from all of them. I would also like to thank
my husband, and my family for their ongoing support
and encouragement.*

Dianne Evans Kelley

This book is dedicated to Amanda and Adam Wied.

Judith Walker-Wied

*I would like to dedicate this book to my loving and supporting family:
my husband, Scott Beckwith; my parents, Dennis and Nancy Forjan;
my son, Sawyer Beckwith; and my brothers, Dave and Jeff Forjan.
Thank you for the continued encouragement in all aspects of my life.
All of you bring me so much joy and inspiration. I would also like to thank
my past and present students, colleagues, and friends.
Without all of you, I would not have had the extraordinary
experiences to aid in cowriting this book. This whole experience
has meant so much to me.*

Kristin M. Forjan Beckwith

Common-Sense
Classroom Management

for Special Education Teachers
Grades 6–12

Jill A. Lindberg • Dianne Evans Kelley
Judith Walker-Wied • Kristin M. Forjan Beckwith

Skyhorse Publishing

Copyright © 2007 by Corwin Press
First Skyhorse Publishing edition 2015

Skyhorse Publishing books may be purchased in bulk at special discounts for sales promotion, corporate gifts, fund-raising, or educational purposes. Special editions can also be created to specifications. For details, contact the Special Sales Department, Skyhorse Publishing, 307 West 36th Street, 11th Floor, New York, NY 10018 or info@skyhorsepublishing.com.

Skyhorse® and Skyhorse Publishing® are registered trademarks of Skyhorse Publishing, Inc.®, a Delaware corporation.

Visit our website at www.skyhorsepublishing.com.

10 9 8 7 6 5 4 3 2 1

Library of Congress Cataloging-in-Publication Data is available on file.

Cover design by Michael Dubowe

Print ISBN: 978-1-63450-318-1
Ebook ISBN: 978-1-5107-0090-1

Printed in China

■ Contents

■ Contents

■ Preface

Dear Teacher,

The field of special education is full of responsibilities, demands, and decisions, and as a new teacher (or a teacher new to the field), you may feel overwhelmed by all you have to do. In addition, the newly revised Individuals with Disabilities Education Act (often referred to as IDEA 2004 or IDEIA), as well as No Child Left Behind, place further demands on special education teachers. This book was written to provide you with useful ideas and suggestions to help alleviate some of the stress you may feel as you meet these challenges. If you are seeking a text that provides help in teaching specific curricula, in demonstrating competence in core subject areas, or in obtaining certification, this is not the book for you. However, if you are prepared in the aforementioned areas and are looking for a teacher-friendly resource to use in your classroom—whether you teach alone or coteach with a general education teacher—you've come to the right place.

The strategies and ideas you find here address some of the most urgent concerns you will face such as specially designed instruction, legal responsibilities, positive behavioral supports, and working with families, to name just a few. Because we know most special education teachers don't have the luxury of reading a book cover to cover and need to be able to find an answer to vexing questions as quickly as possible, we have taken care to make this book very user-friendly. With the busy teacher in mind, each strategy is limited to five points or fewer, and chapters were designed to "stand alone." So, as questions or concerns arise, you need only to turn to the chapter that addresses your specific concern to find a comprehensive list of strategies as well as additional considerations related to the topic. In addition, we will frequently refer you to other sections of the book where you can find out even more information. We also provide you with additional resources. You will also find that the suggestions provided in the book can be implemented without extensive interpretation or planning, creation of materials, or permission from your administrator. They cover many aspects of teaching students with disabilities and provide very specific and practical ideas.

We realize, of course, that schools vary from city to city and system to system and that districts implement special education laws in slightly different ways. However, we know that many needs and concerns are common to all teachers in this field no matter where they are. We think you will recognize some of your own needs and concerns in this book. Keep in mind that these strategies can and should be changed or modified to fit your particular situation. They are not written in stone and should be seen only as a means to an end in assisting you in your ongoing efforts to provide your students with a quality education.

This book is a great resource whether you are a novice special education teacher, someone new to the field, a special education teacher trainer, or a mentor teacher. These clear, easy-to-implement strategies will assist you in meeting the many challenges you face daily and help to ensure ongoing success throughout the school year.

Good Luck!

Jill A. Lindberg
Dianne Evans Kelley
Judith Walker-Wied
Kristin M. Forjan Beckwith

■ Acknowledgments

We thank Claudia Weaver Henrickson, a district administrator known as a Special Education Leadership Liaison, and Peggy Holtman, a special education supervisor, for reading our manuscript and providing feedback on accuracy and clarity of the information. Their experience and vast knowledge of the intricacies of special education helped us produce a quality product.

We also thank Erin Witty, a seasoned districtwide, itinerant, secondary-level special education teacher. She read each chapter to ensure that we addressed the most crucial aspects needed to be an effective special education teacher.

The publisher thanks the following reviewers for their contributions to this book:

Kathy Amacher
Special Education Teacher
Franklin Middle School
Geneva, IL

Sandra E. Archer
National Board Certified Teacher
Ormond Beach, FL

Jo Bellanti
Director, SPED Division
Sullivan County Schools
Bartlett, TN

Mariann C. Carter
NBPTS Certified Exceptional Needs Specialist
Office of Exceptional Children
South Carolina Department of Education
Columbia, SC

Debi Gartland
Professor of Special Education
Towson University
Towson, MD

■ About the Authors

Jill A. Lindberg has a bachelor of science degree in Exceptional Education from the University of Wisconsin-Milwaukee. She retired from Milwaukee Public Schools in June 2003 and is currently a supervisor for the University of Wisconsin-Milwaukee. Her teaching experience includes working for six years as a mentor teacher assisting both regular and special education teachers in Milwaukee Public Schools. She also taught students with specific learning disabilities for four years in a full-inclusion setting and students with emotional/behavioral disabilities for five years, all in Milwaukee Public Schools. In addition, she spent four years in the Madison, Wisconsin, public school system teaching students with hearing impairments.

Jill coauthored *Common-Sense Classroom Management: Surviving September and Beyond in the Elementary Classroom* and *Common-Sense Classroom Management for Middle and High School Teachers* for Corwin Press as a result of her experiences with fledgling educators who struggled with classroom management. As a special education teacher, she wanted to write a book for new special educators and for veteran teachers new to the field.

Dianne Evans Kelley is an assistant professor in the special education department at Cardinal Stritch University in Milwaukee, Wisconsin.

Previously, she worked for 20 years in the Milwaukee Public School district where she taught middle school-aged students with emotional/behavioral disabilities for 10 years, worked as a mentor teacher to beginning special education teachers at the secondary level, and was a program support teacher. Dianne has been an educational consultant since 1989 and has presented at the local, state, and national levels on such topics as positive behavioral supports for students with challenging behavior, and classroom management. She has a master's degree in special education and is currently working toward her PhD in Urban Education/Special Education.

Dianne co-authored *Common-Sense Classroom Management for Middle and High School Teachers* for Corwin Press.

Judith Walker-Wied is Problem-Solving Facilitator for Milwaukee Public Schools, working with teacher teams, administration, and parents focused on student achievement. She has worked with the school district for over 30 years. Her previous positions have included special education teacher for students with emotional behavioral disabilities and specific learning disabilities, diagnostic teacher working with the IEP team process, special education supervisor, and mentor teacher with the University of Wisconsin-Milwaukee Special Education Internship Program. She has taught classes at the university level, and spent a summer teaching students with special needs in Southampton, England.

Her educational background includes a BS in Exceptional Education from the University of Wisconsin-Milwaukee and an MS in Exceptional Education and Administrative Leadership, also from the University of Wisconsin-Milwaukee. The topic of her thesis was cooperative learning. She has recently earned her doctoral degree in Urban Education at the University of Wisconsin-Milwaukee, specializing in Exceptional Education with a focus on teacher mentoring. She has a profound conviction that student achievement can best be supported through teacher collaboration in professional learning communities.

Kristin M. Forjan Beckwith attended the University of Wisconsin-Oshkosh, where she majored in special education with an emphasis on early childhood exceptional needs and learning disabilities. Two full years of classroom experience were included in her training, and she worked in various settings. These included classes for students with specific learning disabilities and cognitive disabilities as well as early childhood classes for children with special education needs. She also worked in regular education classrooms. She taught in Milwaukee Public Schools for seven years, working with elementary students with specific learning disabilities and students with emotional behavioral disabilities. In 2002, she received a master's degree in curriculum and instruction with an emphasis in language arts.

Getting Organized

S pecial education teachers may have a classroom of their own, share space with other special educators, or have a corner in a general education classroom, hallway, or other area. No matter what your situation, you need to be organized—especially if you are a traveling teacher. With the large amount of paperwork and other data for which special education teachers are responsible, having a system that makes sense and keeps important information handy is essential.

Chapter Outline

- Student Information
- Supplies and Materials
- Your Desk and Surrounding Areas
- Forms and Schedules
- Room Arrangement
- Wall Displays

Student Information

Do you feel as though you need a secretary to keep yourself organized? Paperwork responsibilities can be overwhelming, and for that reason you need to find a system to help you keep current with your many duties. (Please note that Individuals with Disabilities Education Improvement Act of 2004 [IDEIA] states that short-term objectives in Individualized Education Programs [IEPs] can be eliminated for all but a small group of students who take alternative

assessments on the basis of alternative achievement standards. However, be sure to check with your school district to see whether it plans to implement this directive.)

▶ 1. IEPs are the most important documents you will draft and refer to throughout the year. Keep them in a safe place that is easily accessible to you. IEPs for all of your students should be in place by the first day of school. If you are missing any IEPs, inform your principal or the special education administrator in your school immediately. The IEP cover page provides a great deal of student and family data as well as the all-important IEP due dates. Make certain these dates are accurate, current, and in compliance with your district and state regulations or laws. Goals and objectives should be written based on your district standards. Double-check all IEPs for behavioral issues, transition goals, transportation, and other supplementary aids and related services that are required for the goals. If you have questions or feel you need assistance writing IEPs, ask your special education supervisor or another member of the special education administration staff in your building. IEPs are legal documents for which you are responsible. Be sure they are done correctly.

▶ 2. Having easy access to necessary student information is very important. If you are teaching students under the age of majority, be sure to have the names of family members or a guardian who has the legal right to make school and health care decisions for the student. Include current home address, home and work phone numbers, and the times when the person can be reached at these numbers. Record the name of another person who can be called in case of emergency. In addition, know the correct last names of family members, as they may not be the same as the student's. You may also want to include the student's birth date, ID number, or any other information that might be useful to you when having a phone conversation about the student with a support staff member or supervisor. Store this information in a secure yet easily accessible location. It's also a good idea to lock up these confidential documents whenever you leave the classroom.

▶ 3. Behavioral information regarding your students should of course be included in the IEP. Be sure you read and understand the specifics, especially if you are responsible for implementing a formal Behavior Intervention Plan (BIP). A BIP is a individualized and detailed plan of action developed to support the student in learning more appropriate behaviors. (See Chapter 4, Positive Behavioral Supports, and Chapter 7, Legal Issues, for more information.) Behavioral information may include a detailed explanation of what the student has responded to in the past and the type of incentive program that has helped the student to be successful, as well as other positive behavioral supports. You may want to make copies of IEP behavior pages for yourself and any general education teachers or support staff involved with the student. If a formal BIP is in place, each staff member involved should have a copy or have access to it and should understand how the plan will be implemented. In addition, be sure you and any involved general education teachers and support staff are aware of serious behavior issues students might have in order to ensure the safety of other students and adults in the classroom.

▶ 4. IEP snapshots are a great way to have necessary student information at your fingertips and to share this important data with your general education colleagues in an easy-to-read format, such as Figure 1.1. The special education administrator in your building or school district may have a form for you to use. If not, you may wish to use the one provided here or create your own.

▶ 5. Many students with disabilities have varying degrees of medical needs that teachers should be made aware of. Before you disclose confidential information, however, find out your district policy regarding the distribution of medical and health information. Your school should have on file any essential medical information such as the name of the student's doctor and who (including parent, guardian, and school staff) has permission to administer medication or medical assistance. Some students take medication at home rather than at school, and there may be times when, for whatever reason, they do not get it. You may want to keep a record of this so you can work with the student (if appropriate), parents, or guardians to ensure the medication schedule is followed. Often, school performance is affected by medication or lack thereof. In addition, take note of any side effects that may result from the medication. You will also want to keep on hand any information regarding therapy a student may be receiving outside of school if families have shared this with you and have given you permission to speak with the therapist. You can usually obtain parental permission forms from your school psychologist, social worker, or your administrator. Also note that some students with disabilities may have special classroom needs. Be sure you are aware of these and make arrangements to accommodate them.

Supplies and Materials

Sometimes it's a real challenge for special education teachers to obtain supplies. But part of your job is to be a strong advocate for your students' rights to the same education using the same materials as their counterparts in the general education classroom. Keep that in mind if you feel apprehensive about asking for what you and your students need.

▶ 1. As you begin to gather supplies and materials, make sure to get copies of all the current textbooks and teachers' manuals you will need for teaching your students. If you have students at different grade levels, then you will need materials for all the levels. Your administrator should be aware of your needs and supply you with these things. However, this might not always be the case, and you may need to borrow from your colleagues or even make copies of some of the materials. Become familiar with what will be taught from these texts in the general education classroom so that whether you teach students separately in an alternative setting or within the general education classroom, both you and your students with disabilities will always be as up to speed as possible. Be sure to check out the teachers' manuals, as many of them offer suggestions for reteaching and modifying work for students who need extra practice. Some manuals may also include an audio tape of the text that can be used to accommodate students with reading or vision difficulties.

Figure 1.1 IEP Snapshot

IEP Snapshot for _____ Special Ed. Teacher _____ Date _____

Present Level of Performance in Academic IEP Goal Areas:

*Behavior Goals/Formal Behavior Plan?   Yes ☐   No ☐

Reading _____

L/A-Writing _____

Math _____

Other _____

Student's Strengths: _____

Supplementary Aids and Services Needed in Regular Education Setting?   Yes ☐   No ☐

	Frequency/Amount	Conditions	Location of Services

Special Factors   ☐ Behavior   ☐ Limited English Proficiency   ☐ Communication

Comments: _____

*If applicable, please see attached Behavior Intervention Plan or other information re: behavior.

SOURCE: Adapted from M. Nieves-Harris, M. S., 2004.

► 2. In addition, seek out any other professionals in your building who can offer assistance with curriculum and teaching strategy information. In some districts, there are content specialists who can offer techniques and strategies as well as materials you can use. This person may even be willing to demonstrate for you or even teach a lesson with you. In addition to content area specialists, most high schools have a department chair for each curricular area. This person can also be a valuable resource for obtaining materials and providing suggestions.

► 3. Special education teachers often use many different materials to support the learning of their students and are always on the lookout for places to find what they need. Teaching supply stores now offer many items that can be helpful. Some of these include supplementary workbooks in all subject areas that provide additional instruction and practice, teacher resource books that provide suggestions on how to adapt work for students with disabilities, and grade-level content books written at lower reading levels. Highlighting tape, graphic organizer templates, and age-appropriate manipulatives are just a few examples of other useful items. Be sure to see what is available at these stores—and take a paper and pencil along to make some notes. You might be able to create some of these things on your own and save some money in the process. Be sure to keep files of everything you purchase or create yourself because they will be useful through the years.

► 4. Ideally, students will come to class prepared with necessary materials; however, this may not always be the case. To avoid lost instructional time, keep on hand a supply of pencils, calculators, extra copies of textbooks, and so on for students to use during the class hour. It's also a good idea to have extra lined paper available. Also, be sure you anticipate activities that require additional supplies (science lab materials, dictionaries, and so forth), and have them on hand and organized before your lesson. Valuable learning time will be wasted if you are scrambling for materials while your students wait.

► 5. Any good behavior management system requires not only planning but supplies as well. No matter what grade level you are teaching, you will probably use some type of consumable incentive. If you know what grade levels you will be teaching in the fall, spend the summer hunting for bargains at drug stores, dollar stores, and garage sales. If you buy a little at a time, the strain on your wallet will be much less. It may even be possible to obtain free certificates for small edible items from fast-food restaurants if you tell them you are a teacher. In addition, you may have a schoolwide incentive program where you teach. Try to incorporate this into your own reward program to stress the importance of following school rules at all times.

Your Desk and Surrounding Areas

Is your desk a frightening and mysterious expanse that you are loathe to conquer? Do you fear you've ignored something very important lying at the bottom of the heaps of paper you haven't the courage to explore? An organized desk area is so important—read on for some valuable advice on how to accomplish this.

▶ 1. It is important to keep your desk surface area as clean and organized as possible. A busy day often means a messy desk as there is usually little time to organize while you are teaching. Take a few minutes at the end of the day to clear away and put things where they belong. You may want to place things that you need to deal with the next day on the front of your desk. If you can manage to organize at the end of every day, you will feel more prepared when you come in the next morning. Remember that your clean desk can be a model for your students as it sends a message that the teacher is organized.

▶ 2. As special education teachers, we have a good deal of paperwork responsibility beyond preparation for teaching. For this reason, finding a system to organize this information is very important. Using baskets, totes, or other compact containers is one good way to do this. Consider designating a shelf for these receptacles or an area on your desk. If you put them on your desk, think about using stackable containers to avoid clutter and to ensure a clear workspace. Listed below are some ways to use your containers and to divide your paperwork so that you are better able to keep things up-to-date. You may think of other ways.

a. Things to complete today—for example, IEP invitations, adaptations to assignments, and correspondence

b. Instructional materials—for example, worksheets for current lessons for individual students or groups

c. Ongoing paperwork—for example, IEPs, behavior plans, and behavioral assessments

d. Contact information—for example, student phone numbers, outside agency numbers, and numbers for supervisors

▶ 3. Make your desk as functional as possible with classroom-necessary items at your fingertips. Your desktop should hold containers with paper clips, pencils and pens, and so on. Also have available a stapler and staple remover. Find a small basket for scrap paper and sticky notes. Keep additional pencils and pens, staples, tape, and other items in a top drawer that is handy for you. A calendar of some kind is another important item to have on your desk. Write down all importance dates including IEP meetings, conferences, report card due dates, and so on for easy reference. Some teachers like a small calendar that can be carried from classroom to classroom, while others prefer a large monthly calendar big enough to use as a desk pad. Whatever you prefer, don't omit this important item to help you keep abreast of daily, weekly, and monthly obligations.

Your desk or whatever space you have should be off limits to students. However, because some students may not comply with this directive or the room may be used by others, make every effort to maintain privacy by writing notes regarding students cryptically, such as using initials only and storing confidential material in a drawer that can be locked, if possible.

▶ 4. Your desk should have a file drawer where you can keep folders for each of your students that contain IEPs, cumulative folders, and other important information. This drawer should lock, as it contains students' private information. You may also want to make files for other school-related information that is important to you. These might include bulletins and communiqués from your principal or the office, items from your special education administrator or supervisor, school policy information, committee materials, and any other things you may want close at hand. If you work in various classrooms, you may also want to keep a folder for each one to hold things you need to know such as upcoming tests, special activities or trips, or other information from the general education teacher. If you don't have a file drawer, consider purchasing a plastic filing container to store this information. Because it is portable, however, it should be stored in a locked area whenever you are not in the room.

▶ 5.   You say you don't have a desk or space of your own? Discount stores usually have rolling carts or file-type drawers on wheels that can work very well and are not too expensive. Ask a colleague or administrator if your school has funds allocated for teacher materials. If not, make this one-time purchase yourself, and think of it as a career investment. Rolling carts and files cabinets can be pushed to any area you may temporarily call home and will provide you with an organized way to carry your supplies and needed information with you. Items to keep in your traveling cart include: lesson plans for classes you may be teaching or coteaching, extra supplies to lend out to students, graded work to return to students, teacher editions, positive reinforcers, discipline referral forms, and a backup lesson plan—just in case.

Forms and Schedules

Teachers—especially special education teachers—are inundated with forms and schedules. Finding a way to make these user-friendly and useful is important. Here are some ideas.

▶ 1.   Depending on the grade level you teach and the setting in which you teach, such as an inclusive classroom or a more restrictive setting, your students' schedules may be quite similar or very different, so you might find it helpful to create a master list of all of your students' schedules. Not only will this help you create an agenda for yourself that ensures services are provided to all students on your IEP list, but it also can be a quick way to direct students who may have forgotten their daily schedule.

▶ 2.   Refer to your IEPs to make certain you are providing services to your students for the time period indicated on the IEP. Students may be served in an inclusion setting or a resource setting where teachers work with individuals or small groups of students. If you work with students outside the general education classroom, do your best to make sure you are teaching content that is aligned as closely as is practical to the general education curriculum so your students can keep up as much as possible. If you are supporting students within the general education classroom, make sure it's at a time when they can really benefit from your help. For example, if a student only requires direct special education support in math, you will want to schedule time to be in that particular class. Sometimes, it takes real thought to create a schedule that involves each of the students you serve in his or her IEP goal areas, especially if you have students in many different classrooms. See the section "Developing Your Schedule to Support Students," in Chapter 3 for some helpful ideas.

▶ 3. To save time in your busy day, make forms and templates that can be reproduced and used again. Use lists that can be checked off or circled to save time rather than repeatedly writing tedious notes. Create forms for behavior reports, notes home, and meeting schedules. Using different colored paper for different forms or academic areas makes it easier to quickly access what you need. Also, develop a form or template for your general education teachers to complete that provides you with information about what will be covered in their classrooms each week. Figure 1.2 is one example of this form.

▶ 4. You may also want to create a template for your weekly schedule. Share this with the general education teachers in your teaching unit so they are aware of the days you will be directly supporting students in their classrooms, the days you will be involved in IEP meetings, and where to contact you in case an immediate concern arises. You should also give a copy of your schedule to others who may need to keep in touch with you, such as paraprofessionals, administrators, and supervisors.

Room Arrangement

If you have a classroom—or perhaps a corner to call your own—it is imperative that you make economical use of the area. Even if your space is limited, you must still serve your students efficiently. So, you need to be organized—here's how.

▶ 1. When setting up your room or your work area, it is important that materials and equipment are easily accessible with adequate space for maneuverability. Your chalkboard, dry-erase board, or overhead screen should be visible from all seating areas. You may wish to set up an area for small-group activities as well as some separate areas for those students who need an area with limited distractions to complete their work. If you have computers, they should be separate but visible from all areas so that you can monitor students' activities there.

▶ 2. To make transition into and out of your classroom as quick and efficient as possible, materials on your shelves should be easily accessible and organized in a logical manner. Labeled baskets or bins are commonly used organizational tools. Depending on how you are providing services to students, you may want to have separate baskets for each class hour or each subject area.

▶ 3. Designate an area of your shelving to be used as a resource center and include items such as encyclopedias, dictionaries, thesauruses, grammar guides, and specific topic-related materials based on what your students are currently studying.

▶ 4. If you are traveling from room to room, staying organized is a special challenge. Using a rolling cart or file drawer on wheels that can be stocked with materials you need for each class can be a practical way to stay prepared (see above under "Your Desk and Surrounding Areas"). Keep supplies for different classes in separate containers so you can quickly transfer them to your cart—and off you go, prepared and organized for your next lesson.

Figure 1.2   Class at a Glance

Teacher _____ Week of _____

Academic information for following class(es) _____

To identify areas in which students will need assistance, please provide a summary of lessons to be taught for the week.

READING

Title of Book: _____ Pages to read _____

| In class assignments during the week? | ☐ Yes | ☐ No | Days _____ |
| Homework during the week? | ☐ Yes | ☐ No | Days _____ |

Comments: _____
_____

WRITING/LANGUAGE ARTS

| In class assignments during the week? | ☐ Yes | ☐ No | Days _____ |
| Homework during the week? | ☐ Yes | ☐ No | Days _____ |

Comments: _____
_____

MATH

Assignment Pages_____

| In class assignments during the week? | ☐ Yes | ☐ No | Days _____ |
| Homework during the week? | ☐ Yes | ☐ No | Days _____ |

Comments: _____
_____

ADDITIONAL COMMENTS _____
_____
_____

Thank you, your input is appreciated,

Special Education Teacher

Wall Displays

Organized teachers use wall displays to provide consistency and structure throughout the school day. Items to display include informational postings, visual cues, and instructional content. But what if you don't have a wall? If you haven't guessed by now, special education teachers need to be creative. Here are some suggestions for what to post and how to post whether you have a wall or not.

▶ 1. Informational postings let students know what is expected of them. Suggested postings include: classroom rules and consequences; course materials list; hourly bell schedule; emergency procedures; and a calendar of key dates such as exam dates and vacation days. Items that should not be posted include students' grade point averages, personal contact data, and any other information that should remain confidential.

▶ 2. Many students with disabilities rely on visual cues to help them remember what to do or how do to things. Some examples include learning strategies for reading, writing, and math; multiplication tables; and examples of how to properly label work to be submitted. To further strengthen the effectiveness of visual cues, consider using different colors as well as graphics such as arrows.

▶ 3. Even if you have limited space to call your own, it's still important to find a way to display pertinent information. If you work in general education classrooms, most pertinent information will already be posted. However, you might want to ask your coteacher for bulletin board or wall space to post additional information that will assist the students with disabilities.

▶ 4. Some special educators travel from classroom to classroom throughout the day to provide instruction and support within the large group via coteaching or by working with a small group within the general education classroom. In these instances, you may need display space for instruction (post the lesson agenda, vocabulary words, and so on). However, there may be insufficient time available to write all this down on the board before you begin the lesson. The following are some suggestions that will enable you to include visuals in your instruction without using valuable instructional time.

    a. Most classrooms have an overhead projector. Prepare your transparencies prior to instruction. You can handwrite or use your computer to type the lesson and print the transparencies directly from your computer's printer. If you have not created them from a computer printer before, read the box carefully to make sure you purchase the type that is compatible with your printer.

    b. A trifold display board (sometimes used in science projects) is sturdy enough to stand upright on its own yet is portable as it can be folded when not in use. You can buy sticky gum at most drug stores or teaching supply stores to mount things temporarily on these boards. Because items can easily be attached and removed, you can reuse the board for different lessons.

    c. A portable whiteboard is another option. Use a dry-erase marker to record lesson content on the whiteboard prior to the class. Then, when it's time to teach, lean the whiteboard up against the chalkboard or drill a hole at the top of each end and string sturdy cord through the holes so that the whiteboard can be hung from a map hook.

d. A highly portable alternative to the whiteboard is the *Instant White Board Office Edition.* You can place these 2" × 3" plastic static film sheets anywhere because they stick to any surface. As with the traditional whiteboard, you can write on these with a dry-erase marker, wipe off when finished, and reuse. When not in use, the sheets are rolled up and stored in a tube. You can order this item from the following Web site: www.presentationresources.net.

e. The use of technology in the classroom is on the rise. Document cameras, LCD projectors, and Smart Boards are just a few examples of technology that can be powerful instructional tools yet require little setup time. Find out what technology is available in your school and make a point of learning how to use it.

2

Organizing Students

S taying organized can be a monumental task for many students, but for those with disabilities it can be especially challenging. Teaching your students how to do this will save them—and you—time, frustration, and wasted energy. Knowing how to be organized is an important life skill, and your time will be well spent if you help your students learn to do this.

Chapter Outline

- Preparing for Class
- Storage Systems
- Daily Organizational Strategies
- Routines and Rules
- Peer Buddies

Preparing for Class

Are you frustrated by the amount of time it takes to prepare yourself and your students for class? Remember that disorganization is a huge time waster. If you feel this could be an issue for you and your students, here are some proven ways to handle the problem regardless of whether instruction takes place in a special education environment or within the general education classroom.

> 1. If you share space or travel from room to room, it's very important to keep materials organized and accessible. To make sure you are ready to teach, no

matter where it may be, store daily supplies in a movable cart. Keep this cart stocked with paper, pencils, and other necessary supplies. Learning time is wasted when students wait as you rummage and search for supplies, lesson materials, and so on.

▶ 2. A stitch in time saves nine. In the teaching profession, this can easily be translated to mean that finding a way to inform students of needed supplies and materials for class will save learning time. Then students wouldn't need to go to their lockers to retrieve forgotten homework or borrow spare textbooks. List all needed supplies for the class hour on a small whiteboard and hang it just outside your classroom door or some other place where it will be highly visible to students. Instruct them to review this list before going to their lockers. If a whiteboard is impractical, consider writing daily supplies on a laminated sheet of paper. Take this time-saving organizational tip one step further by listing everyday supplies, such as paper and pens, in permanent marker. Then use a dry-erase marker to add specific supplies for the day, such as a silent reading book, calculator, and study guide. You may also want to collaborate with others in your teaching unit and generate a complete list of needed materials for all classes.

▶ 3. Of course, you should encourage your students to be independent and responsible young adults. However, the reality is that some students with disabilities have a difficult time coming to class prepared. If this is a regular occurrence, there will most likely be a goal page in the Individualized Education Program (IEP) addressing this concern. As you and the student work toward reaching this goal, it's a good idea to have a backup plan in place if the student is chronically unprepared. Allowing students to sit with nothing to do during the hour because they neglected to bring their supplies is not an effective strategy toward remedying this behavior. Equally ineffective is to give the student a hall pass to retrieve forgotten supplies as it wastes learning time. Suggestions to save time and maximize learning include having supplies available for loan or sale, keeping a few extra copies of textbooks for students to check out, or even allowing supplies to be stored in your classroom at the end of the class hour or day. Try building in a positive reinforcement program to encourage students to come prepared to class, and consider developing a supplies and materials checklist with the student that can be inconspicuously posted in his or her locker or stored in a folder.

▶ 4. It's often beneficial to build in a few minutes at the end of the class hour to allow students to wrap up and get organized for the next class. Provide a variety of suggestions on staying organized, and encourage them to choose a method that works for them. Color coding folders with matching book covers, using a large binder with several folders, or keeping a daily planner in which to jot down assignments are just a few suggestions. Depending on the severity of the student's disability, ongoing assistance for staying organized may be necessary.

▶ 5. In addition to wrap-up time at the end of each class hour, set aside time at the end of each week or two to help students deep clean their binders, lockers, and so forth.

Storage Systems

If you teach in a resource room or more restrictive classroom setting, you may want to use a storage system to help students stay organized. Wire baskets, stacking cardboard mailboxes, and hanging folders are just a few suggestions. This strategy offers some tips on how to get the most out of a storage system.

▶ 1. Regardless of the storage system you elect to use, develop a clear and easy-to-follow labeling system. A storage system won't be effective if students can't figure out where they should file homework, pick up worksheets for the class, and so on. As you plan, take a few moments to determine the best location for the storage system. To increase the likelihood of students remembering to check it as they enter and file items as they exit, you will want to consider a spot near the door. However, you may want to avoid placing the storage system so close to the door that you end up with a traffic jam as students enter and leave the room.

▶ 2. Until it becomes a routine, position yourself near your storage area to remind students to pick up and drop off items as they enter and exit the classroom. You may even want to post a chart above the storage system for students to check in assignments as they submit them. Because of concerns regarding privacy, you may choose to assign students a permanent number and have them check in their work under their number rather than their name.

▶ 3. If your class sizes are small enough, you may be able to assign each student a mailbox. While enabling the students to be better organized, this system can also be very convenient for you. For example, rather than taking class time to return completed work or distribute journals, these items can be directly filed into each student's mailbox. Individual mailboxes can also be used to hold assignments and school information distributed during a student's absence. You may even decide to hire a responsible peer to gather and file the assignments for the absent students.

▶ 4. If having individual student mailboxes is not a practical option, you may want to consider designating mailboxes per subject area, class hour, or whatever seems most logical. For instance, stackable wire baskets can be useful for collecting and sorting student work throughout the day. Simply label each basket (hour 1, hour 2, and so on). Then direct students to place homework in the appropriate class-hour basket as they enter the classroom and to deposit any completed in-class assignments as they exit.

▶ 5. Hanging files are another alternative to individual mailboxes. One suggestion is to label them by subject and class hour, and then place three differently colored folders within each hanging file using labels such as *homework, worksheets for today's class,* and *extra copies* (for students who were absent or lost their copy). You may choose different labels. Another option is to assign each class a different hanging file—for example, brown for algebra or blue for English. Take this organizational tool one step further and use two hanging files per class. Label one, *completed work* and the other, *while you were out.* Assign one student to collect completed work from everyone and to place it in the appropriate hanging file. Ask a second student to gather any worksheets and record the assignments for those students who are absent and place them in the *while you were out* file.

Daily Organizational Strategies

Many students with disabilities also attend general education classes, and good organizational skills are a necessity for success in those classes. Bear in mind that organizational strategies are only helpful to a person if they make sense to them—what works for one person is not necessarily effective for another. Our job as teachers is to present several different organizational strategies to students, and then guide them toward creating a method that works for them.

▶   1. Binders can be a useful tool in helping students with disabilities organize their days. They're a good choice not only because they enable the student with a disability to be better organized but also because most students (those with and without disabilities) use them. The following are just a few suggestions for helping students make the most of this organizational tool.

    a. To help students create a useful binder, brainstorm helpful features to look for. Encourage students to choose organizers that have a Velcro or zipper closure, several pockets in which to store supplies such as calculators, a ruled edge, and so forth. The binder should also have three rings in which to secure three-holed pocket folders.

    b. "I forgot my assignment." Aside from "The dog ate my homework," this is one of the most frequently used excuses for coming to class unprepared. To decrease this behavior, suggest that students have one pocket folder per subject. Direct students to place work to be completed in the left pocket and work to submit in the right pocket.

    c. Binders should also have several pockets to hold daily supplies as well as materials for lesson accommodation such as learning strategies written on index cards, a multiplication chart, daily report, and hand-held spell checkers. To preserve the privacy of the student, accommodation materials within the binder should be as discrete as practical. For instance, some students with disabilities use the marks on a ruler to help add or subtract. One alternative to a plastic ruler is to place a 12-inch piece of ruler tape on an inside edge of the binder. This product cannot be found in teaching supply stores but, although designated for a different purpose, works well in this case. The best way to locate this item is to search online using the key words *ruler tape.* You should find several online shop sites.

▶   2. Color coding materials is another organizational strategy helpful to many students with disabilities. Have students wrap textbooks in colored paper covers that match corresponding subject folders. If students would rather not wrap their textbooks, another option is to use different colored *Highlighter Tape* (Lee Products Co.). Because this tape is removable, it will not damage textbooks. Or purchase small round color coding labels from an office supply store. Students can then place like-colored labels on the corner of each folder or notebook as well as on the outside binder of each wrapped textbook. You may also suggest that students jot "1 of x, 2 of x," and so forth on each circle to further cue them as to how many materials they need for each subject.

▶   3.   Most computer-generated course schedules are confusing for teachers to read, and even more so for many students with disabilities. Help students break these highly cryptic codes by providing them with an easy-to-read version of their schedule that highlights only the classes they are currently attending. In addition to the class hour and subject, other pertinent information that should be included on the schedule are the days of the week the class meets (if other than every day), the teacher's name, the room number, and the name of the textbook for the class. Remember to update this schedule as course schedules change throughout the school year. See Figure 2.1 for a schedule template.

▶   4.   Learning strategies such as mnemonic devices, visual cues, or other strategies to help remember processes can also be useful in teaching a student to be better organized. A good resource to find organizational learning strategies is "The Learning Toolbox" (http://coe.jmu.edu/LearningToolbox/index.html). More information on learning strategies can also be found in the section "Learning Strategies" in Chapter 6.

Routines and Rules

Most students need and appreciate the structure that classroom rules and routines help provide. The key, however, is to be consistent in their use. Consider the following suggestions:

▶   1.   Routines and rules must be established and posted in your classroom to create consistency and an orderly environment. Establish your own routines on the basis of scheduling and your teaching style and follow them as much as possible so your students know what to expect. If you work only with small groups somewhere in the general education classroom or other small spaces, this still applies. See Chapter 1 for ideas on how to find wall space or post your rules on the back of an extra chair if that's all the space you have. Haphazard routines and inconsistency in following classroom or group rules can negatively affect your students' ability to learn.

▶   2.   Let your students help create your classroom or group rules as this will encourage them to take ownership—but try to have no more than five rules. Be sure the rules are measurable and observable, and state them in the positive. For example, "Ask permission to leave your seat" rather than "Do not get out of your seat unless you ask the teacher." Just as academic skills need to be taught, classroom procedures need to be taught to students as well. Sharpening pencils, entering and exiting the classroom, and passing out papers are just some of the classroom routines you may want to regularly review with your class or group. Depending on the special education needs of your students, you may want to physically practice procedures to provide additional instruction.

▶   3.   Review classroom or group rules hourly or daily until you are confident your students understand them—even if this takes a month or so at the start of the school year. Do this periodically throughout the year to help ensure ongoing appropriate behavior. Don't assume that one effort at the beginning of the year will last until June. Provide copies of your rules in contract form to be signed by each student—and consider sending one home for family members to review, sign, and return. This will place even more emphasis on the importance of meeting your classroom or group behavior expectations.

▶   4.   Keep in mind the old adage that "the only thing for sure is that nothing is for sure." Schedule changes are sure to happen due to teacher absence, special programs, or other events. It's good practice to keep students informed of upcoming events and schedule changes as some students with disabilities—students with autism, for example—may have difficulty with change. Try to give your students as much notice as possible about variations in their routine. Post any daily changes along with the hourly class agenda on the board or other spot in your room that is easily seen. Take a moment to review these things at the start of the class.

▶   5.   Often, students with disabilities are involved in several different special education services and other activities throughout the week. To help students be in the right place at the right time, encourage them to keep a copy of their weekly schedule. Resource time with the special education teacher, occupational therapy, meetings with a transition specialist, piano lessons, and so forth should be noted on their schedule.

Peer Buddies

As a special education teacher, you have duties almost too numerous to count, and the most important one is to help ensure the academic success of your students. If you don't have an adult teaching assistant, consider using the buddy system to further support students.

▶   1.   Peer buddies can assist students in several ways. They can help with daily organization, act as academic tutors, clarify questions, or provide cues to help the student with a disability follow along with classroom instruction. Peer buddies should not be used as a friendship-building strategy. Friendship cannot be forced, and it is not fair to either party.

▶   2.   Before you implement a peer buddy support plan, thoughtfully consider every aspect. Foremost, begin by asking the student with the disability how he or she would feel about having a peer buddy. Be honest and clear about the roles and expectations of each student. If the student declines, you may want to gently prod to see if there is a specific concern that can be remedied. However, the final decision is the student's, and you should respect his or her wishes. If you are considering a student without a disability as peer buddy to a student with a disability within the general education classroom, look for a relatively good academic student who is mature and gets along with others. If you teach in a resource room or more restrictive classroom, you may be able to work with a general education teacher to have some students come to your room—or space—to help for an agreed upon period of time. It is extremely important to remember to respect student privacy; carefully think through how you will be able to offer support through the use of a peer buddy without disclosing private information.

Figure 2.1 Daily Schedule

Student name: _____

Semester: _____

Mark Period: _____

Class Hour	Class Days	Room #	Subject	Teacher	Textbook & Other Supplies
1					
2					
3					
4					
5					
6					
7					
8					
9					
10					

▶ 3. You will want to talk with both students to be sure they clearly understand the purpose of the pairing. Be honest but sensitive in discussing the reason with them, and provide only necessary information to the peer buddy. Both students should understand that when they work together it should not be a time for socializing and that the role of the peer buddy is to support and reteach, not to do the work for their peer. Establish a periodic check-in with them to be sure things are going as planned. You may want to inform the parents of the classroom buddies about this program. Assure them that all students involved will benefit and that no one will miss out on any learning time.

▶ 4. If things are not working out well between the two students, don't force the issue. Meet with the students to see whether you can assist in working through the problem. Sometimes it's a quick fix, such as clearing up a miscommunication or reviewing roles. If either one of the students, however, decides that it isn't working out for them, dissolve the team. Then if need be, consider finding a more compatible pairing.

▶ 5. To encourage harmony and effort on the part of the students who are in your peer buddy program, you might want to include an incentive for participation. In some schools, peer buddies can earn credit for their participation. If that is not the case where you teach, consider incorporating participation into their course grade. You may also opt to provide an occasional reinforcer, such as a pizza party, for all peer buddies.

3

Delivery of Special Education Services

A special education teacher has a great deal of responsibility and accountability beyond classroom teaching. Although identification of disability and decisions regarding delivery of services are made by an Individualized Education Program (IEP) team, the special educator is often looked to as the expert in the field. Not feeling like "the expert?" This chapter will help you to feel more confident in assisting the team with making sound decisions and will provide you with suggestions for ensuring provision of services throughout the school year.

Chapter Outline

- Determining Level of Educational Services for Students With Academic Disabilities
- Determining Level of Support for Students With Behavioral Challenges
- Providing Educational Services
- Developing Your Schedule to Support Students
- Sharing Student Information
- Providing Services to Students With Disabilities Through Collaboration
- Special Education Instructional Planning

Determining Level of Educational Services for Students With Academic Disabilities

Students with disabilities must be provided with access to the general education curriculum and with the opportunity to receive their education within the general education classroom to the greatest extent appropriate.

While the general education classroom is the ideal placement, the IEP team must consider the unique needs and strengths of the individual student to determine the level of support the student requires and to identify the most appropriate place where services will be provided. Following are considerations for determining appropriate special education services and supports.

▶   1.   The IEP team first determines areas in which a student requires special education services. Following that determination, the team should then consider where services will be provided and who will provide them. For instance, some students with disabilities will be able to receive special education support within the general education classroom; others may spend the greater part of the day in general education classrooms with some time outside of it to strengthen skills or work on specific deficit areas. Other students require a specially designed environment and curriculum for most of the school day. If it has been determined that the student will attend general education classes, the team will decide how much direct support is necessary from the special educator. For instance, some students may require accommodations that could be implemented by the general educator. However, some students, typically those with more significant learning or behavioral disabilities, may need the special education teacher to work directly with them to make progress. In making these determinations, the team considers the student's strengths and areas of need in relation to the least restrictive environment.

▶   2.   Students with a disability who are functioning near grade level can often participate in the general education curriculum with only limited academic or instructional accommodations. With students who are working at this level, a special educator may not need to be in the general education classroom.

▶   3.   Students whose skills are considerably below grade level may also attend general education classes the majority of the school day. However, these students will most likely require additional services. The type of services required is determined by the needs of the individual student. Following are suggestions for providing services.
   a.   The special educator may provide direct services to the student within the general education classroom through coteaching or academic adaptations.
   b.   A special education paraprofessional or teaching assistant may work with the student within the general education classroom.
   c.   The student may have scheduled time in a special education resource setting.
   d.   The general education curriculum may be modified to allow the student to participate, although to a lesser extent than nondisabled peers.

▶ 4. A small percentage of students with a disability will have limited access to the general education curriculum due to skills that are significantly below grade level. These students may spend most, if not all, of their school day working within a special education classroom. Although the IEP team may have determined that the student's needs can best be met within the special education setting, the team should explore opportunities within the school day when the student can meaningfully be included within the general education classroom.

▶ 5. Delivery of services as indicated in the IEP should be reassessed periodically to ensure that the student is receiving appropriate adaptations and support from special education. Any changes to required services should be noted on the IEP. Be aware that IDEIA provides more flexibility for parents and schools by allowing them to agree to make minor changes in a child's IEP without reconvening the IEP team. However, be sure to check with your school district to determine how IEP revisions will be implemented.

Determining Level of Support for Students With Behavioral Challenges

Students with behavioral challenges may or may not require academic adaptations in addition to behavioral support. For those students whose primary need is in the area of behavior, the following information can help the IEP team determine the most appropriate level of behavioral support. As with considerations for providing access to general education curriculum, IEP teams should strive to include the student in the general education setting to the greatest extent appropriate.

▶ 1. Some students with behavioral challenges are able to fully participate in the general classroom with minimal environmental changes or behavioral adaptations. In addition, providing these services may not require direct support from a special education teacher. To make this determination, the IEP team should ask:
   a. Is the student's behavioral challenge "under control"? A student such as this may be able to consistently maintain appropriate behavior and may only need a limited amount of outside support from special education, such as time at the beginning or end of the day to touch base with the special education teacher.
   b. Has the student learned how to self-monitor his or her behavior? Self-monitoring is a powerful instructional technique. Many students can learn how to keep their behavior in check with this instructional technique. See the section "Providing Indirect Behavioral Support to Students in the Inclusive Classroom" in Chapter 4 for information on how to teach a student to use self-monitoring.
   c. Is the student placed in general education classrooms in which the teachers employ best practices that encourage appropriate behavior? Good teachers often build in classroom management programs, focus on positive and preventive strategies, and hold high expectations for students. These built-in supports are often sufficient to reduce inappropriate behavior.

d. Would academic adaptations decrease the likelihood of inappropriate behavior? Some students demonstrate inappropriate behavior because they are struggling with academic demands. Consider whether academic adaptations to lessen frustration and to allow fuller participation would be beneficial to the student.

e. Would behavioral adaptations such as preferential seating and periodic breaks assist the student in demonstrating appropriate behavior? For instance, the student may need to sit near the teacher so he or she can provide periodic redirection, or the student may need to be seated in an area with limited distractions. Short breaks that allow the student a chance to get out of seat to expel energy or take a short time-out from a frustrating task may also be necessary.

► 2. Some students can successfully participate in the regular classroom setting with modifications, such as opportunities for time out from the regular education setting as needed, scheduled resource time to focus on learning social skills, direct special education support, or a Behavior Intervention Plan (BIP).

► 3. A small percentage of students may demonstrate such significant behavioral challenges that they require a special education environment for most, if not all, of the school day. For instance, some students may benefit from an environment that has limited distractions, a smaller teacher-to-student ratio, or a highly structured setting. When making this determination, the IEP team should consider building in opportunities for the student to be included within the general education setting. This will provide occasions for the student to learn more appropriate behavior from peer models.

► 4. When determining appropriate access to general education curriculum, delivery of services as indicated in the IEP should be reassessed periodically to ensure that the student is placed in the most appropriate setting.

Providing Educational Services

Your job is to ensure that every student on your caseload receives special education and related services as described in the IEP. Devising a plan to meet all of your students' unique needs can be tricky, but not impossible. Following are some suggestions for doing so:

► 1. First, review your students' IEPs to identify pertinent information. Figure 3.1 provides an organizational form you may wish to use. Regardless of whether you jot this information on notepaper or use the form provided, the following should be included:

a. *The level of support needed*—For instance, does the student require direct (face-to-face contact) or indirect support, such as consultation between special and general education?

b. *Where services will be provided*—Note whether the student receives special education services within general education classroom, the special education classroom, or both settings.

c. *Specific areas of need*—Identify specific curricular areas such as reading, writing, or math and testing accommodations as well as specifics regarding behavioral support.

Figure 3.1   Student Information Form

Student _____

Predicted Grade Level for Fall 200 _____: _____   **ID#** _____

Area of Need: Behavioral support   Academic support

Present Levels of Academic Performance

Reading _____   Math _____

Written Language _____   Spelling _____

Student's current placement and level of support:

☐   Fully included in general education with _____ % of direct contact with special education
     teacher

     Subject areas for direct support: _____

☐   Partially included in general education

     _____% of time in general education

     Subject areas for direct support: _____

     _____% of time in resource classroom

     Subject areas in resource room: _____

☐   Self-contained placement _____% of school day

     Included in general education setting for: _____

Additional comments:

_____

_____

_____

_____

▶ 2. For high school students—and perhaps some middle school students—beyond the information provided in the IEP, you will also want to find out the specific courses the student must take to graduate, prepare for postsecondary education, and so forth.

▶ 3. The information gathered can then be used to ensure students are provided with appropriate schedules and services. Schools use a variety of methods for scheduling students. Following are four of the more common scheduling methods as well as considerations for each:

    a. In some schools, all student schedules are created via a computerized program. The computer program may take particulars into consideration such as content to be taught outside of general education, but usually students are randomly assigned to classes on the basis of their grade level, course requirements, or other criteria. Schools may choose this method as a way to ensure that students with disabilities are not treated differently from their peers who are nondisabled. A potential downside to this method, however, is that students with disabilities may be placed in several different classes, thus requiring considerable creativity and collaboration among educators.

    b. A second scheduling option—more commonly used in middle school—is to assign all students on the special educator's caseload to one teaching unit. Students with disabilities are then distributed equally across all home bases. For instance, if a teaching unit is composed of four academic content teachers and 20 students with disabilities are included within the teaching unit, each home base would have five students with disabilities. The general and special educators collaborate to determine how and when students with disabilities receive their special education services. A model such as this may be used because it adheres to a best practice recommendation for inclusive education in which no more than one-third of the classroom is composed of students with disabilities (assuming there are at least 25 students assigned to the typical secondary level classroom). However, for this model to be effective, teachers must be highly flexible and possess good collaborative skills.

    c. Similar to the second option, but probably more applicable to high school, is to assign one special educator to each department; for instance, one special educator may work with the math department, another special educator may work with the English department, and so on. Because students with disabilities may be receiving services from several different special educators, these teachers must collaborate with one another to ensure services are provided to all students with disabilities across the content areas in addition to collaborating with the general educators in their department.

    d. A scheduling option that allows for more control in providing services is to group students with disabilities on the basis of needs and level of services. For instance, students who require the greatest amount of special education support may be scheduled together in one class, while students who need less support are placed in other classes within the unit or department. With this model, the special educator spends the greater part of his or her day in classes with students who need more services, while providing a lesser amount or perhaps indirect support to the rest of the students on his or her caseload. Because students are grouped with others who have similar needs, this scheduling method may be considered by some in the field as "tracking," a term that often has a negative connotation. You should therefore consider the pros and cons of this scheduling method.

Developing Your Schedule to Support Students

Once your students' schedules have been established, your job is to develop an agenda that will enable you to provide the special education services noted on the IEPs for all of your students. If you are furnishing services to students primarily within the general education setting, devising a schedule to ensure services for all students can be quite an undertaking. Developing a workable schedule will require creativity and flexibility not only from you but also from the general educators in whose classrooms the students are placed. Following are suggestions to help you work through this daunting task:

▶ 1. There are many factors that will influence how you create your schedule, including the grade level(s) you are teaching, the number or students on your caseload, and the level of support your students require. Consider developing a coded graphic organizer that notes each student's schedule, the content areas in which students require special education support, and the amount of time and level of services needed. For instance, next to the student's name, you might record an "R" to signify needs in the area of reading, and an "M" for needs in the area of math. A star may be used to signify areas in which the student requires direct special education instruction.

▶ 2. Because your schedule revolves around the needs of the students, it will probably look different each school year. Be aware, however, that it may need to be revised each semester and even perhaps each marking period. With this in mind, you will want to review your schedule periodically throughout the school year to ensure you are adequately meeting the needs of all your students.

▶ 3. Figure 3.2 provides examples of commonly used schedules. As you can see from example 1 in Figure 3.2, the special education teacher supports students across three classes during one class hour. If you choose this schedule, you will want to consider the following:
    a. *The amount of time you will need to spend in each class*—For instance, will you divide your time equally across all three classes, or will you need to spend more time in one class due to factors such as course content or IEP requirements?
    b. *Schedule flexibility*—Will it vary day to day depending on class activity, or will it remain relatively consistent?
    c. *Your role in each classroom*—Although you will want to have an active role in each class, your level of involvement may be limited by the amount of time you spend in each classroom. To allow opportunities to coteach, consider whether it's feasible for you to occasionally spend more time

with one class. For instance, could you spend the first 30 minutes of a 50-minute class coteaching with one teacher, and then divide the remainder of your time checking in on students in the other two classrooms?

d. *Weekly planning meetings with the general education teachers*—You will need to meet with the general education teachers to get lesson plans for the upcoming week so that you can determine in which classrooms you will need to be and when you will need to be there. In addition to devising your schedule, you may also need time to adapt work for students in classes in which you may not be present.

e. *A consistent method of sharing your schedule with teachers and students*— Everybody should have a copy of your weekly schedule that notes when you will be working in each classroom as well as where you are throughout the day should an immediate concern arise. It's also a good idea to provide the office with a copy of this schedule.

Figure 3.2   Sample Scheduling Form

Example 1: Hourly Schedule

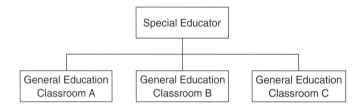

Example 2: Daily Schedule

Period 1 Classroom A

Period 2 Classroom B

Period 3 Classroom C

Period 4 Teacher lunch

Period 5 Classroom D

Period 6 Varied support

Period 7 Preparation hour

Example 3: Weekly Schedule

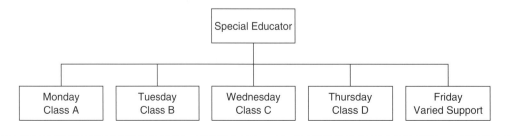

SOURCE: Dieker (2001) and Walsh & Jones (2004).

▶ 4. Example 2 is that of a daily schedule (Walsh & Jones, 2004). As you can see, the special educator spends one class hour a day with each of the general education teachers within the department. Teachers may use this model at the middle school level, when students who require more direct special education instruction travel together from class to class, or similarly at the high school level if the special educator is not assigned to a content area department. One hour a day is commonly left open to provide individualized services. This might include having students come into a resource room or having the special education teacher work with individuals or small groups of students within the general education setting. Considerations with this model include the following:

a. *Your level of participation in each classroom*—Even though you will want to have an active role in each class, it would be unrealistic to attempt to team-teach with each teacher in every classroom on any given day. A more practical option might be to team-teach with one or two teachers each day, and then participate in the other classrooms to a lesser extent. This could include supporting students by circulating around the classroom during the lesson or reteaching a small group following instruction provided by the general education teacher.

b. *Your collaborative relationship with colleagues*—Although you are there for the students, one of the best ways to support them is to build and maintain a good working relationship with your general education colleagues. That said, you might want to vary your level of participation in each classroom to avoid the perception that you are doing more in one classroom than another.

c. *Regular planning meetings with general education colleagues*—Set aside a regular time to meet with all general education teachers to get lesson plans for the upcoming week as well as to plan for your instructional role.

▶ 5. The third format (adapted from Dieker, 2001) is a weekly schedule in which the special educator works within a teaching unit. An example of this would be in the middle school level or within a content area department at the high school level where the special educator spends an entire school day with one teacher. Fridays are left open to provide additional support to individual students either in the general education setting or in a resource setting. Although a model such as this provides the opportunity for coteaching, factors to be considered include:

a. *General educators' confidence in working with students with disabilities*—All the general educators you are working with must feel comfortable providing academic adaptations and dealing with behavioral issues that may arise on the days you are working in another classroom.

b. *Provision of services to the students in their other classes*—You will need to collaborate with the other teachers in your teaching unit to ensure that the needs of the students with disabilities are being met. This may mean that the general educator provides accommodations, that you develop adapted work for the general education teacher to give to the student, or that a teaching assistant or paraprofessional assists in the classroom. You may also decide to excuse yourself for a few minutes either at the beginning or end of each class hour to check in with another class, provide IEP services, and so forth.

c. *Discussion with general education teachers to determine your role in instruction—* Factors that will impact your level of involvement include your knowledge of the content area, comfort level of both you and the general education teacher regarding coteaching, and the amount of planning and preparation time available prior to instruction.

Sharing Student Information

The IEP needs to be implemented from the first day of the school year. Therefore all staff members working with the student need to be familiar with its contents. It is your responsibility as the special educator to review the IEPs of all the students on your caseload and share pertinent information with others. Although this task may seem daunting, you can accomplish it with relative ease by answering "Who, what, and when." Read on for suggestions about how these three "Wh" questions can help you share information efficiently and effectively.

▶ 1. The first question to consider is "Who needs the information?"
  a. Because they are partners in implementing the IEP, all general education teachers working with a student with disabilities should have access to pertinent information. Keep in mind that the teacher may need more than just content-specific information. For instance, the geometry teacher will need information regarding adaptations for math; however, adaptations for other content areas such as reading or writing might also be needed as math course work will most likely include reading and writing.
  b. Other teachers who may need IEP information include fine arts or vocational teachers. For instance, fine arts or vocational teachers would need to know math adaptations noted on the IEP. Also, all of these teachers would need to be made aware of any behavioral adaptations in place for a student.
  c. Others who may require information regarding the student's IEP include teaching assistants working with the student and administrators who may have an active role in supporting the student.
  d. Students should also be provided information regarding their IEP. Regardless of whether they plan to attend a postsecondary institute or find a job right after high school, they need to be aware of the adaptations required to compensate for their disability and those required to maximize their abilities. This information will enable them to learn how to advocate or to make adaptations for themselves throughout their life.

▶ 2. The second question is "What information needs to be shared?"
  a. Pertinent IEP goals and benchmarks (if appropriate) should be shared with any staff working with the student. Please note that IDEIA states that short-term objectives can be eliminated for all but a small group of students who take alternative assessments on the basis of alternative achievement standards. Because states and districts can choose whether or not to implement this recommendation, make a point of finding out your school district's policy.

b. Academic and behavioral adaptations necessary for students to make progress on their IEP goals must also be shared. If the student has a BIP, this document should also be shared with others working with the student.

c. Share the student's strengths as well as preferred learning style with general education teachers as this information will allow them to build in opportunities for the student to use his or her abilities.

d. Be sure general education teachers are aware of accommodations to state- and districtwide assessments. Although most students with disabilities will participate in the same testing as students without disabilities, a small number will not take state and district tests because of the severity of their disability. The general education teachers should know the assessment status of each student with disabilities in their classroom.

e. Specific medical information may also need to be shared. For instance, you may want to note whether the student carries an inhaler for asthma, is prone to seizures, or needs to be excused at a certain time of day to take medication. Be careful, however, about disclosing confidential information. It's a good idea to talk to others in your school, such as other special educators, the school nurse, or administrators, to determine what is appropriate to share.

▶ 3. The third question to consider is when information is to be shared. As previously noted, the IEP needs to be immediately implemented. There are, however, other times of the school year at which IEP information needs to be distributed. Following are considerations to help you keep on top of this responsibility:

a. Because students' schedules often change each semester or possibly each marking period, remember to provide a copy of important information to the upcoming classroom teachers. You may want to write a note on your calendar as a reminder to distribute this information before the first day of the new session.

b. Periodically, a student's schedule may change during the semester. This may occur because of a scheduling conflict or a change in level of special education services. In this event, the general education teachers will need a copy of pertinent information to prepare for the incoming student.

c. IEP meetings are held throughout the school year. For instance, they are held to reevaluate eligibility, to develop an annual IEP, and to revise a current IEP. Make sure general education teachers are provided with an updated version of the IEP following any meetings in which changes to the IEP have been made.

Providing Services to Students With Disabilities Through Collaboration

Collaboration is defined as a style of interaction in which two or more professionals work together toward a common goal (Friend & Bursuck, 2002). Most special educators rely on collaboration with others as a means of providing education to students with disabilities. For instance, as special education teachers, we not only collaborate with general educators and fellow special educators

but also often depend on a strong collaborative relationship with parents, paraprofessionals, related service providers, and our administrators. Read on for suggestions to facilitate collaboration.

▶   1. Special education teachers often collaborate with one another to ensure consistency in service delivery to students with disabilities across grade levels, subject areas, or certain times of the day. Following are examples of collaboration among special educators:

a. One special educator may provide specially designed math instruction to students with disabilities in a resource setting while another special educator supports the other students with disabilities in their general education classrooms.

b. Teachers with specialized knowledge in teaching students with autism, hearing loss, vision loss, and so forth may provide suggestions, resources, and/or materials to other special educators working with these students.

c. Toward the end of the school year, the special education teacher working with freshmen students with disabilities may forward IEP snapshots to the special educator working with sophomores. See Figure 3.1 in this chapter or Chapter 1, Figure 1.1, for sample snapshots.

d. Special educators may also collaborate with one another across different schools. For instance, at the end of the school year, a middle school special education teacher may forward information to the high school special education teacher who will be working with the student the next school year. Similarly information regarding a student transferring from one school to another during the school year may also be shared between teachers.

e. At the high school level, the IEP teacher may collaborate with the transition specialist to determine and develop appropriate work skills and related vocational experiences that will assist the student with transition beyond high school.

▶   2. Effective special education teachers realize the value of establishing a good collaborative relationship with parents. Make a point of introducing yourself early in the school year to the parents of your students, and keep the lines of communication open throughout the school year. Parents should not only be kept in the loop regarding their child's progress and concerns you may have, but should also know about their child's successes or improvements. It's a good practice to keep a record of your parent contacts, and a contact log can be found in Chapter 8, Figure 8.3.

▶   3. Special and general educators collaborate on a regular basis. For instance, collaboration is required to identify needs and services during the IEP meeting as well as to determine delivery of services to students with disabilities within general education. Following are a few suggestions on collaborating with general educators:

a. Because general educators must be aware of their designated responsibilities for implementing the child's IEP as well as any accommodations, modifications, and supports that must be provided, make sure they have access to the IEP. Another option is to provide them with an IEP snapshot (Figure 3.1, or Figure 1.1 in Chapter 1).

b. Although general education teachers are important members of the IEP team, they may not be comfortable with their role. It might be helpful to

offer some guidelines as to what they should be prepared to discuss at the meeting. (See Figure 3.3 for a list of guide questions).

    c. Students with disabilities who are learning in an inclusive setting may attend classes with several different general educators. It's often impractical and possibly intimidating for parents and the student to have all of the student's general education teachers attend an IEP meeting. If this is the case, you may want to ask the other teachers on your teaching team to jot a few notes on the form provided in Figure 3.3 prior to the meeting. During the meeting, these notes can be shared to ensure all voices are heard.

    d. General and special educators also need to collaborate to determine appropriate instructional techniques and behavior management for the general education classroom. Additional information on these topics as well as more information on collaboration and coteaching are provided in Chapter 5.

▶   4. As a special educator, you may also need to collaborate with related service providers, such as physical or occupational therapists, school psychologists, or speech pathologists.

    a. The IEP will designate what services are provided. Devise a way in which you and the specialist(s) can coordinate efforts to implement the IEP. For instance, the physical therapist could provide suggestions on how you can build in opportunities throughout the school day for a student to strengthen his or her fine motor skills. Also, don't forget to establish periodic meetings to talk about student progress.

    b. At the high school level, an outside service provider with whom you may collaborate would be the Department of Vocational Rehabilitation (DVR). This person may have a different title in your school district. Since DVR is a public agency that provides resources to students and assists them with postsecondary vocational skills, you will want to invite a representative to attend and participate in the student's IEP meeting.

▶   5. You may have a teacher assistant assigned to work with the students with disabilities within the general education classroom or within a more restrictive setting. Regardless of where the assistant is working, keep in mind that this person's job is to provide special education services to students—not to help the teachers with copying or other busy work. Therefore, the teaching assistant should spend most of his or her time working with students. If the assistant is supporting students within the general education classroom, meet with this person and the general education teacher(s) to discuss the assistant's role within the classroom and how students can benefit from his or her help. Create a schedule and provide a copy to the assistant as well as to all teachers who will be working with that person.

Special Education Instructional Planning

As a special education teacher, your duties may be more varied than your general education counterpart. In the same hour you may be teaching one student, a small group, or an entire class. Having a format that can help you frame your lesson(s) can be very helpful. Consider the following conceptual framework for effective instruction (Ysseldyke, Algozzine, & Thurlow, 2000, p. 198)

Figure 3.3 General Education Teacher Guide for IEP Team Meeting

Student_____ Date of report_____

Teacher completing form _____

1. How is the student's attendance in your class?

2. What are the student's interests?

3. Describe the student's work habits and motivation.

4. How is the student's behavior in your class?

5. Explain how this student functions during unstructured time.

6. Describe the student's peer and adult interactions.

7. Do you have any behavioral goals for this particular student? If yes, what are they?

8. What is the student's current level of functioning? Describe academic weaknesses or strengths.

9. List 2 or 3 academic goals for your class.

10. List any academic adaptations or behavioral interventions you have utilized in working with the student as well as a brief assessment regarding their effectiveness.

▶ 1. Whether you are working in the general classroom or with a group of students with disabilities, effective instruction is paramount. It is important to have a framework to use each time you plan your lessons to help ensure that you carefully consider how you will manage each part. The following conceptual framework for effective instruction is applicable regardless of the number of students you are instructing.

▶ 2. Plan for instruction. First, decide what to teach by identifying your lesson objectives. Then, consider the learning requirements of your students with disabilities. If you are teaching one student or a small group, you can easily target your instructional planning to the students' IEP goals. If you are teaching a whole-group lesson in the general education classroom, determine how you can relate lesson objectives to the IEP goals for your students with disabilities.

▶ 3. Manage the instruction by deciding what methods you will use to teach the lesson. As you plan, consider the students' different learning styles. Whenever possible, include visual, auditory, and kinesthetic components to your lessons. Repeating key points, providing examples, and demonstrating procedures on the board are just a few suggestions. You can also address different learning styles by varying the presentation of the content and types of activities. For instance, in addition to teacher-directed lessons, build in opportunities for students to work in pairs and or in small groups.

▶ 4. Deliver the instruction with an eye to student comprehension. Read your students' faces. What do their expressions tell you? Are they focused? Do they appear uninterested or perhaps confused? Build in opportunities to check comprehension and clarify points throughout the lesson. Pause periodically to ask students to restate what they've heard or work problems while you circulate to check understanding. Don't move on if you think there are a number of students who are confused. If it appears that only a select group of students is struggling with the content, plan to review the material later with that particular group of students. If you are teaching in a general education setting, don't be surprised to find that your review group may not only include students with disabilities but students who are nondisabled as well.

▶ 5. Evaluate the instruction throughout the lesson, especially when students are working on a new concept. Assess individually as you circulate around the classroom or as you monitor your group. Pair a strong student with one who needs extra help or guidance, but check on them as they work to be sure they are on task. Watching students work individually can be a valuable way of assessing the effectiveness of your lesson.

Positive Behavioral Supports

4

S tudents who demonstrate inappropriate school behaviors often challenge even the most seasoned teachers. Developing strategies to effectively address these behaviors not only will have a positive impact on teaching and learning, but will also ensure a safe learning environment. The strategies in this chapter will help you handle many of the behaviors you may encounter.

Chapter Outline

- Classroom Management and Coteaching

- Providing Indirect Behavioral Support to Students Within the Inclusive Classroom

- Managing Behavior in the Special Education Classroom

- Addressing Individual Student Behavior Challenges

- Managing Special Education Classrooms Designed for Students With Extremely Challenging Behavior

- Tokens of Recognition and Other Fabulous Prizes

- Activity Reinforcers

- Backup Plans for Students Not Earning the Incentive

- Consequences

- When You Must Discipline

■ Functional Behavioral Assessment and Behavior Intervention Plan

■ Conducting a Functional Behavioral Assessment

■ Developing a Behavior Intervention Plan

Classroom Management and Coteaching

Some special education teachers have the opportunity to coteach with one or two general education teachers a good percentage of the school day. In these instances, both teachers may collaboratively develop and implement the classroom management system. When thoughtfully implemented, coteaching can be one of the most effective classroom management systems. Read on for suggestions on how coteaching can support appropriate student behavior.

▶ 1.　To be a truly effective classroom manager in the inclusive classroom, you will want to establish your credibility so all students will view both you and the general education teacher as equals. One way to do this is to share responsibility for classroom management. To avoid situations in which you and your coteacher may not be disciplining the same way, build in time during planning to establish behavioral expectations and consequences for infractions. Make a commitment that neither of you will make changes without consulting the other, and present these expectations to the students as a team.

▶ 2.　One of the benefits of coteaching is sharing responsibility for teaching and managing classroom behavior. For instance, when one teacher is leading instruction, the other may take a greater role in managing behavior. Although this is a commonly used type of coteaching—typically with the general educator in the lead teaching role—be careful not to assume the role of bouncer or helper teacher on a regular basis. To avoid this pitfall, demonstrate a united front and communicate with each other in front of the students. For instance, if a behavioral concern arises during class, take a moment to meet privately—out of students' earshot but within their eyesight—with your coteacher to discuss and strategize. Once you have reached consensus on how to address the concern, as a teaching team, meet with the student. If it's not possible for both of you to talk with the student or if you are concerned that the student may feel he or she is being "ganged up on," determine who will talk with the student. When meeting with the student, use language to convey your united front. For example, you may say something such as: "Ben, Mr. Andrews and I talked and feel that despite several warnings and opportunities for you to change your behavior, you have continued to disrupt class. We have decided that the next course of action is for you to meet with Mr. Collins about your behavior." Referring to your coteacher as well as using words such as "we" rather than "I" reinforces that you are a team.

▶ 3.　To help students with disabilities succeed within the inclusive classroom, you and your coteacher should consider strategic seating assignments. For instance, if you have students who exhibit challenging behaviors, seat them in an area surrounded by others who have good self-control and a more positive school attitude. If you have students who are functioning below grade level, consider seating them near peers who are able and willing to provide some occasional assistance. On the other hand, you may have a student who works better by him- or herself—someone who is easily distracted by others or who likes an audience. You may want to consider giving this student some space by finding a seat away from others or assigning a seat where a minimal number of students will be distracted by this person's behavior.

▶ 4. Make sure the students with disabilities understand the classroom rules, routines, and structure. To help students learn appropriate classroom behavior, take time to clarify rules, provide frequent review of expectations—especially prior to transitioning—and consider using private cues or signals such as a light tap on the desk to cue a student back to task.

▶ 5. You and your coteacher should do your best to make sure that the students with disabilities are an integral part of the general education classroom. They should be fully involved in all classroom endeavors. Lessons and instructional activities should be planned with ability, cultural, and gender diversity in mind. To ensure that this happens for all students with disabilities, you might need to include academic adaptations or create specific behavior management plans to enable them to be part of the class.

Providing Indirect Behavioral Support to Students Within the Inclusive Classroom

There may be classes in which you spend very little time. Perhaps you are only in the room for a part of the class hour or only a few days a week. In these instances, you may not have much input into classroom management and must follow the management system set up by the general educator. Even if your contribution toward developing the classroom management system is minimal, you still play a crucial role in ensuring proper behavioral supports for students with disabilities. The trick is to devise things that can be easily implemented by the general education teacher when you are not present. Or better yet, encourage the student to become responsible for his or her own behavior.

▶ 1. Students who are prepared with materials and who have completed their assignments are less likely to create problems in the classroom. Disruptive behaviors can escalate when students ask to leave the room to retrieve assignments or if they are unable to participate in the lesson because they don't have their textbook. Whether or not you are in the classroom with your students, you need to be sure they can keep track of their supplies. Devise a system—colored pocket folders for each subject, a homework sheet on which assignments can be written, a checklist of materials taped to the inside of the student's binder, extra pencils available for sale or loan, and regular locker cleanings are just some recommendations. See Chapter 2 for more suggestions. Although these are simple ideas, they can be very effective ways of helping students stay on track.

▶ 2. Take a few moments to assess the current classroom management system to determine whether minor adaptations would assist the student. Following are some guide questions and considerations for minor changes:

a. Does the teacher periodically remind students of behavioral expectations throughout the lesson? If so, are these reminders more often stated positively and proactively? Here are some examples: "Thanks again everybody for working so quietly with your lab partners," or "Be careful class. I am starting to hear some off-task conversations, and remember, I am collecting this assignment—complete or not—at the end of the class hour." Statements such as these not only encourage students to maintain appropriate behavior but also forewarn students of impending consequences.

b. When redirecting students, does the teacher use blanket statements such as "It's getting loud in here, please remember that in order to listen to the radio at the end of the class hour, we all need to be working quietly"? Although providing frequent reminders and redirections is good practice, some students with disabilities may not understand that this redirection also includes them. Sometimes they have difficulty processing oral directions or comprehending vaguely stated comments. So consider whether a more explicit and personalized directive such as "Josh, remember that the class is working toward earning time to listen to the radio the last 10 minutes of class. Please stop talking to Max and get back to work."

c. Do the students with disabilities also require nonverbal cues to help them comprehend? For instance, the teacher can point to the clock to signal the student that he or she is wasting work time, use proximity to redirect the student, devise a private cue such as a finger to the lips to signal the student to be quiet, or even place a small egg timer on the student's desk to indicate how long he or she must work on a particular task. If signals are not being used, consider whether the student could benefit from a nonverbal cue such as the previous examples. If the teacher uses nonverbal cues, make sure the student knows what the signal means, as some students with disabilities, such as a nonverbal learning disability or autism, may not understand the connotations behind a cue.

d. How often is the incentive issued? If the reward is too far in the distance for the student, he or she may lose interest or may be unable to maintain the behavior. If this appears to be the case, consider whether the student can earn tokens or small incentives leading toward earning the larger reward. For instance, if the class is working to earn a pizza party at the end of the marking period, perhaps the student who needs additional behavioral support could earn a ticket for each day he or she meets behavioral expectations. A predetermined number of tickets would be required to participate. You may also want to consider adding bonus incentives if the student exceeds the number of required tickets.

▶ 3. You may find that some students with disabilities who are demonstrating more challenging behaviors require more intensive support than provided by the current classroom management plan. This doesn't necessarily mean that an entirely different plan must be developed for these students. If there is a solid classroom system in place that works for most, consider whether adding an individualized plan will help the student make better behavior choices. For instance, a written contract developed by you, the student, and the general education teacher may help the student take responsibility for his or her behavior. Hold a brief meeting to determine the desired behavior, criteria for success, and an agreed on incentive. Once all of you have come to an understanding, the contract should be signed by all, and a copy should be given to the student.

▶ 4. Self-monitoring is an individualized behavioral management system that empowers a student to make a change in behavior. Direct instruction from a teacher is usually necessary initially. However, students can easily learn to monitor their own behavior through the use of a behavioral report or by simply using a tally system to denote behavioral incidents. During the instructional period for self-monitoring, the student should be reinforced for accurately counting his or her behavior. As the student becomes more aware of the behavior, the incentive is given at the point where improvement is noted. Follow these steps to establish a self-monitoring management system:

   a. Meet with the student to identify a behavior that needs improvement as well as to agree on an incentive for accurately monitoring the behavior.

   b. To ensure that both you and the student will be monitoring the same behavior, talk about what the behavior looks like or sounds like.

   c. Every time the behavior occurs during class, both you and the student should mark a tally on your individual data collection forms.

   d. At the end of the class hour, compare marks. If the totals are fairly similar, the incentive is given to the student. If the marks are considerably off, talk about why this may be happening. Continue practicing for several more days or until the student becomes more accurate. Once the student understands how to record the occurrence of his or her own behavior, the management system should be successful.

▶ 5. Behavioral reports are useful tools for monitoring behavioral issues. These can be completed daily or weekly, depending on the student's behavior. Sample daily and weekly reports can be found in Figures 4.1 and 4.2. To use a daily report, write the behavioral goals for the day on the bottom of the report so all teachers (and the student if evaluating his or her own behavior) are aware of the expectations. At the end of each class period, the teacher or teacher and student should circle the appropriate score earned. At the end of the school day, the student and teacher should discuss the day's behavior in relation to the goals. The student should take the report home to be signed by the parent and returned to school the next day. For students with less severe behavioral concerns, you may opt to send home a weekly report. Depending on the number of teachers with whom the student works, you may choose to have each teacher complete the report, or take a few minutes during common planning time to complete one report as a teaching unit.

Figure 4.1   Daily Progress Report

Student: _____   Date: _____

Please circle the appropriate score for the hour and initial. Take into consideration classroom behavior and productivity

Subject	Score	Teacher's Initials	Comments
	5 4 3 2 1		
	5 4 3 2 1		
	5 4 3 2 1		
	5 4 3 2 1		
	5 4 3 2 1		
	5 4 3 2 1		
	5 4 3 2 1		
	5 4 3 2 1		

5=Excellent
4=Very Good
3=Good
2=Try Harder
1=Poor

Thank you,

Goals:

_____

_____

Parent's Signature

_____

Figure 4.2 Weekly Progress Report

Please take a few minutes to complete the progress report below

Student _____   Week of _____

Teacher _____

Subject _____   Class Hour _____

Comments

Participation	5 4 3 2 1	
Classroom behavior	5 4 3 2 1	
Completion of assignments	5 4 3 2 1	
Quality of work	5 4 3 2 1	

5=Excellent   4=Very Good   3=Average   2=Below Average   1=Poor

Additional comments:

_____

_____

_____

Managing Behavior in the Special Education Classroom

If you are teaching in a resource room or in a special education classroom you will need to devise your own classroom management plan. This plan will depend on whether you are teaching students coming and going throughout the day— common to a resource setting—or teaching a core group of students for the greater percentage of the school day in a self-contained setting. Universal to any site, however, is the need for discipline, order, and cooperation. There are several things to consider as you plan. Read on for some suggestions.

▶ 1. Sometimes there are students who simply do not get along, and you may find that you are spending more time acting as a referee than as a teacher. If you are providing special education services to students within a resource room, see if it's possible to rearrange students' schedules. Perhaps some students can come to the resource room during a different class hour, or you may be able to exchange students with another special education teacher just for this one class hour. If there is no other option, begin by evaluating your classroom management plan to determine whether you need to make any revisions. Next, develop individual behavior management plans for those students who need additional intervention. Talk privately with each of these students about one behavior you would like changed and the type of incentive they would like to earn. If you are diligent about implementing the plan, expecting compliance, and following through with rewards, you should see improvement. If poor behavior continues or escalates, you may need to develop a formal Behavior Intervention Plan (BIP). (See the strategies later in this chapter that discuss Functional Behavioral Assessments (FBAs) and BIPs.)

▶ 2. Some of the same concerns in the general education classroom can become issues in your classroom, even if you are working with small groups of students. Seating arrangements can be important, so have a strategic plan. Know your students, seat them in a way that promotes harmony, and don't hesitate to rearrange if and when it becomes necessary. Develop some simple, observable, and measurable rules such as the following: stay in your seat, raise your hand to talk, and follow the teacher's directions. Create an incentive system on the basis of points earned for compliance with classroom rules.

▶ 3. Despite your best efforts, there will be times when students will come to class unprepared. Rather than waste valuable instructional time sending students back to their lockers or expecting them to sit and listen rather than participate, keep extra supplies such as pencils, pens, lined paper, and copies of textbooks on hand. You may be able to get some of these things from your school office, or check them out from the school library. If you must shop, look for back-to-school sales at the end of summer; you should be able to stock up on these items at a minimum of cost to you. Your local teachers' convention may give away a variety of useful items, such as pencils, erasers, and pens. Have students check out items for the class hour to be returned to you before they leave the classroom.

▶ 4. You may also want to provide folders to store assignments. Have students keep these in the classroom so unfinished work is not lost. If some students seem to complete assignments faster than others, have a folder of extra credit assignments from which the student can select.

▶ 5. Finally, remember that you must do your best to see that your students have access to the general education curriculum during the lessons you teach. Find materials that supplement what is being taught in the general education classroom. This will help your students feel more connected to the content and to their peers in the general education classroom. For more detailed information about how to do this, see Chapter 5.

Addressing Individual Student Behavior Challenges

The main goal of every teacher should be academic and behavioral progress for each student, but it will be a difficult one to reach if there are ongoing behavior concerns to contend with. Address problems before they escalate and become impediments to learning for all your students. Look below for some ways to get started with this.

▶ 1. Early in the year as you read through the Individualized Education Programs (IEPs) of your students with disabilities, you will undoubtedly find that some have behavior goals. Usually, to address these goals, teachers must create individual or group behavior programs. Keep in mind that they need not be complex and should not be difficult to implement. These programs are informal and different from formal BIPs that are addressed later in this chapter and in Chapter 7. Remember that if you have a classroom management system in place that is used consistently and seems to work with the majority of students, you will have a context within which to develop programs for individual students that will have a good chance at success. Please be advised: For this strategy to work, you must have a positive and mutually respectful relationship with your students. If you have a tenuous relationship with any of your students, this strategy could backfire, causing more classroom turmoil if your students may come to view you as an opponent rather than an ally.

▶ 2. When devising a course of action for dealing with the behavior of individual students, first look to the IEP. The IEP not only should identify specific behaviors the student is working on, but should also note positive behavioral supports in place to address the behavior. If you are following the IEP, and the student's behavior has not improved, it may be time to reconvene the team to review or revise the IEP. Following are a few more recommendations to consider when addressing behavioral challenges:

a. If the student has more than a couple of behavior goals, place priority on any behaviors that have the potential for being dangerous, and then look at other behaviors that most affect the student's ability to function in school. For instance, a particular student's IEP may contain a goal page to address the behavior of leaving the building without permission and another goal page regarding not turning in assignments. In this case, priority should be placed on the unsafe behavior of leaving class without permission.

b. Consider whether an alteration in the classroom or group setting could change the behavior. For example, if a student constantly disturbs or provokes his or her neighbors and as a result cannot stay focused, perhaps moving the student away from the group may improve behavior. If it helps, you have saved time and frustration on your part and helped the student without having to worry about developing a program to address the behavior.

    c. Identify behaviors that seem to be the catalyst for other behaviors. For instance, a student who rummages through your desk, walks in and out of the classroom, and writes graffiti on the bulletin board clearly needs to alter his or her behavior. Rather than addressing each of these separately, look to the root cause of this behavior—getting out of his or her seat. Then, devise a plan to remediate that behavior.

▶   3. Talk with the student about the behaviors that concern you and also about possible incentives he or she would like to earn. Because different things motivate different people, trying to set up a program with no understanding of what motivates the student to improve behavior is a recipe for failure. Find out, within reason, what might influence your student to work to change a behavior. Ask for some input and offer some of your ideas. You can gather this information by interviewing the student, having the student complete an Interest Inventory, or by having the student complete a Forced Choice Survey. Interview and Interest Inventory questions might include such queries as: "What is your favorite sport, food, movie, singer?" or "If you had free time during the class hour, what would you like to do?" or "What is your least favorite subject, class hour, task?" Think carefully about your questions to ensure that you are gathering information that will help you work with this student and to decrease the likelihood of the student offering a less than appropriate response. In fact, you will probably have better results if you meet privately with the student, and let him or her know in advance why you are asking these questions. Forced Choice Surveys are less open-ended as the student is given two choices and asked to pick his or her preference. You can find a program for creating such a survey (also called a reinforcer survey) at Intervention Central http://www.interventioncentral.org/ under the heading On-Line Tools—which you can find on the right side of the main page. Then, click on "Jackpot!: On-Line Reinforcer Survey Generator" and enter the required information.

▶   4. Contracts, self-monitoring, and behavior reports as mentioned earlier in this chapter (see section "Providing Indirect Behavioral Support to Students Within the Inclusive Classroom") are just a few examples of individualized behavior plans. Use one of these or develop your own way to evaluate and monitor the student's behavior. First devise a monitoring system, such as a form on which to keep track of points, or have the student write his or her name on an index card, and use a special stamp or hole puncher to mark the card throughout the class hour. Next determine a specific criterion for success and how and when the incentive will be issued. Suggestions for incentives include coupons good for such things as free time, computer time, lunch with the teacher, and so on. If you want to offer tangible or edible rewards, the list is endless. Popular items include individual serving size bags of snack crackers, cookies, and pretzels as well as cans of soda, fast-food coupons, and candy bars. Be advised, however, if using edible rewards, you should check for food allergies. You might also want to check out discount stores for novelty items that cost a dollar or less. There are also catalogues that sell items of interest to teenagers, such as word search books, fun pens, art supplies, and the like at very affordable prices.

▶ 5. If you have tried the suggestions in this strategy but continue to have difficulties with a student, you may want to enlist help from other professionals in your school who should be willing partners with you in dealing with those students who have challenging academic or behavior problems. See Chapter 9 for some ideas. But remember that to make a credible request for help, you must provide evidence of the efforts you have made and documented to change the child's behavior. Here are some things that should be included:

    a. Begin a daily anecdotal report on the child. It doesn't need to be anything long or involved. You may want to include information on how the rest of the class is affected by the behavior.

    b. Think about the positive reward systems you have in place in your classroom or group, and list them. Comment on how the student responds to them.

    c. List the individual reward systems you have created for the student. Comment on how the student responds to them.

    d. Document problems the student may be having in other classes and settings such as hallways or the cafeteria.

    e. Inform family members, and keep them involved in your efforts. It is very important to make the family aware of the positive things their child does as well as the challenging behavior exhibited. Coordinate efforts between home and school. Don't forget to briefly document what you are doing to involve family.

At this point, you have given support staff members a body of information indicating that you have put forth a real effort to change the student's behavior and that it is time for input from other school professionals. You may also need to consider a formal BIP.

Managing Special Education Classrooms Designed for Students With Extremely Challenging Behavior

Most schools offer a continuum of educational services and supports that meet the needs of all students with disabilities. Even though we should strive to include students with disabilities within the general education setting, the reality is that there are some students with significant behavioral challenges whose needs can best be met in a more restrictive setting. These classrooms often make or break a special education teacher. Read on for ideas of how you can be one of the success stories.

▶ 1. Little learning will take place in a classroom full of chaos and negativity. To help establish a productive learning environment, a positive and consistent classroom incentive program should be in place. Classroom incentive programs are like snowflakes—no two are alike. Whatever program you decide on, you should thoroughly consider these aspects:

    a. *The expected classroom behaviors*—Think this through, as you want to make sure you cover all aspects of classroom management. You and your incentive program will lose credibility with the students if rules are made up as you go along or if changes are continually made during the incentive program. State behavioral expectations succinctly and positively to help students know what they should and should not do.

b. *The reward the students will be working toward*—You may want to survey students to find out what motivates them as they will be more likely to work toward something they want.

c. *The method used to collect and present data*—Your students need to have some tangible way to know they are on the right track with their behavior. Points accumulated on the board, stamps on a calendar, or graphs are some of the ways to visually present this information. But don't forget to tell your students what they are earning and why they are earning it. In addition to keeping your students informed throughout the class hour, it's a good idea to summarize the total points earned at the end of each class.

d. *Realistic criteria for success*—Criteria that are set too high may be unattainable, while criteria set too low will not challenge the students to improve behavior to a more acceptable level. Establish a graduated scale of success with increased incentives for meeting higher criteria. This, too, should be posted for students to see. See "realistic criteria for success" below.

e. *The duration of the incentive program*—The success of your incentive program hinges on the length of time students must perform a behavior before they receive their reward. If it runs too long, students will lose interest or feel the reward isn't worth the wait. If the duration is too short, you will begin to feel like you spend more time rewarding your students than teaching. A good rule of thumb is to run the first couple of incentive programs for about one week. Then once your students have gotten the hang of things and behavior has begun to improve, increase the duration of the incentive to two or three weeks.

f. *The method of explaining the plan, including how often you will review expectations*—One of the more common reasons incentive plans fall apart is lack of communication. The best-laid plans will fall flat if you don't devise a way to explain the incentive program clearly. Students need to be well advised on all of the above elements of the incentive plan. In addition, they need frequent reminders about expectations, feedback on progress, and recognition for their appropriate behavior.

▶ 2. Here's an example of a classroom incentive program using the aforementioned elements. This example runs the length of one week and represents a self-contained setting in which the students are together five class periods a day with each class lasting 50 minutes. If you choose to implement this program, you will need to adjust the number of points possible for classes of different lengths.

a. *The expected classroom behaviors*—
   1. In seats at the bell, quiet and ready to learn.
   2. Work quietly and on task at assigned seat. Verbal reminders such as, "Be careful, it's getting rather loud; I may not be able to give a point this time around," will be given as needed if students begin to veer off task.

b. *The reward the students will be working toward*—Students will work toward earning the Platinum Card status that will afford them the opportunity to watch a full-length movie and be served popcorn and soda. Lesser rewards will be given if students don't meet the highest criteria (see "realistic criteria for success" below).

c. *The method used to collect and present data*—The class will be able to earn up to five points per class hour (approximately one point every 10 minutes). The tallies will be marked on the board, and specific praise will be given along with the points. Daily points will be added toward a grand total. The total number of points possible over the duration of the incentive program will be 100.

d. *Realistic criteria for success*—A graduated reward system will be implemented as follows:

Platinum Card (85–100 points) = full length video, popcorn, and soda party (may require up to two class hours to see entire video)

Gold Card (80–84 points) = video party—no snacks (two class hours)

Silver Card (75–79 points) = one class hour of leisure time activities (no snacks)

e. *The duration of the incentive program*—The incentive program will begin on a Monday and last through Thursday. Points will be collected for four days, and the reward will be given during the afternoon of day five (Friday).

f. *The method of explaining the plan including how often expectations will be reviewed*—Posters reminding students of the behavioral expectations and the graduated reward system will be placed on the front bulletin board. The teacher will spend the first 10 minutes of class on Monday (day one) explaining the entire incentive program to the students. The students will be reminded of the behavioral expectations the first few minutes of each subsequent class hour. At the end of each class, students will be told how many points they earned for the day as well as the grand total to date. Each time points are awarded, the teacher will let students know why they are earning this particular point by repeating the expectation they are demonstrating. For example, "I really appreciate that all of you are working quietly and staying on task. This behavior just earned you a point."

▶ 3. Poor attendance is not uncommon with secondary level students, especially students with behavior disabilities. If you are concerned that students only show up on the days incentives are issued—or even worse, don't show up because they know they cannot participate due to poor attendance—you may want to implement a daily incentive program instead. To kick off this incentive program, begin by stating the expected behaviors for the class. You may want to provide a visual reminder by writing them on the board or pointing them out if already posted in the classroom. Next, explain to students that they as a team can earn points for demonstrating the expected behaviors. However you, the teacher, will earn points when students are not following the expected behaviors. For example, if one of the expectations is for students to wait to be called on before speaking, the student team earns a point each time the class meets this expectation, while you earn a point if someone talks without waiting to be called on. As the goal of this incentive program is to shape and reinforce appropriate classroom behavior— something your students will most likely need to work on—allow students to improve their behavior by giving a warning before you earn a point. Do this by writing a question mark or a dotted tally next to your score. If behavior improves, erase the warning; if not, you earn the point. These points could be used for free time at the end of the day (or over a few times during the day, if students need more immediate reinforcement), time spent listening to the radio while working quietly, or dividing the points equally among the students. Then give them some choices in cashing in to buy a snack or a free pass on one homework assignment coupon. For students who rarely attend school, earning these incentives might give them the opportunity to see what they have been missing and encourage them to attend more regularly. Please be advised, in order for this strategy to work, you must have a positive and mutually respectful relationship with your students. If you have a tenuous relationship with any of your students, this strategy could backfire causing more classroom turmoil as your students may come to view you as an opponent rather than an ally.

▶   4.   Remember, the goal of any incentive program is to establish a positive and productive classroom environment. As you begin your program, you may find the expectations you are setting for your students' behavior may be somewhat lower than you would like. This is acceptable as you want them to feel some success. Once they understand what is expected of them and have improved their behavior, you can raise your expectations as well as the percentage of points necessary to earn the reward. You may also be able to increase the length of time the incentive program runs.

▶   5.   A few more pearls of wisdom . . .
   a.   Be aware that because you are working with students with extremely challenging behaviors, most of your students will probably have BIPs. Before the beginning of the school year, review the BIPs and jot down specifics to use as a ready reference. You will want to make sure that you are addressing each student's challenging behaviors in the most appropriate manner.
   b.   Become a "multitasker." That is, use every activity reward as well as modes of instruction as an opportunity to work on IEP goals, practice social skills, encourage the use of replacement behaviors as noted on a BIP, and so forth. Your students will benefit from the additional opportunities to learn and practice more appropriate behaviors.
   c.   Although a classroom management incentive program will help create a productive and orderly classroom, your responsibility to teaching students with more significant behavioral challenges is far from over. Once classroom order is in place, concentrate on teaching students how to acquire an internal locus of control; that is, owning their behavior as well as learning how to regulate it without relying on external incentives such as tangible rewards or activity reinforcers.

Tokens of Recognition and Other Fabulous Prizes

Secondary level teachers are often quite surprised when their students respond positively to tangible rewards. If it seems immature for them to work toward earning pencils, coupons, and the like, remember that it may not be the reward itself that has meaning but rather the recognition and praise they receive.

▶   1.   Fabulous prizes are all those fun and wonderful items you use as game prizes, raffle winnings, and so on. Stumped as to the kinds of prizes that will motivate your students? Ask them—or have them choose from reinforcer inventories you can find online or in teacher idea books. Fabulous prize ideas that appeal to most students include small bags of salty or sweet snacks, candy bars, fast-food restaurant certificates, books, and magazines. Also, discount stores offer many novelties for a dollar or less, or you can watch for sales on markers, books, and so on at discount stores. There are also catalogues from which trinkets and other prizes can be ordered bulk at very affordable prices.

▶ 2. Pens and pencils are another example of tangible rewards students seem to like. Those with different ink and lead colors, shaped erasers or caps, and other unusual features will likely catch their eye. Don't assume you will have to purchase these items yourself. They can often be found at teachers' conventions, shops, banks, and even military recruiting centers. If you do decide to purchase them, pick up some pencils that have recognition comments on them to give to deserving students.

▶ 3. Coupons can be used to cash in on a variety of rewards from those that are activity-centered to those that are consumables—it's up to you. Some suggestions include coupons that can be cashed in to excuse missing homework or class work assignments, or coupons to participate in an activity such as computer time, free time or game time or to earn a small prize or treat.

▶ 4. Funny money and tokens can also be used as rewards. An incentive program involving these things can be as simple or elaborate as you would like to make it. Decide how and when students will earn and spend their money. Along with earning money, you may also decide to charge students for infractions such as not turning in an assignment or coming to class late. Also, determine what students can buy with their money. Suggestions include activity time, a free homework pass, edibles, and small inexpensive prizes that you can find in a variety of catalogues that sell to organizations sponsoring carnivals, festivals, and so on. Finally, decide if all items are for sale at a flat fee or if items will have varied values. Create a catchy name for your money by calling it Behavior Bucks, or use the school name or mascot such as Cardinal Cash, or use your last name—for example, Kelley Koins. Let your students be part of the process by submitting ideas and then voting on their favorite.

Activity Reinforcers

Tangible reinforcers as mentioned in the previous section are a positive and relatively simple way to recognize or encourage appropriate behavior. Activity reinforcers can be an equally effective reward system. An additional benefit is that these type of reinforcers can also foster positive relationships as well as provide students the opportunity to engage in more intrinsically motivating activities.

▶ 1. Team games not only can be used as a reward for good behavior, but can also be a great way to sneak in a little academic skills review and social skills practice. With a little ingenuity, you can adapt television game shows and board games into activities that can be played with an entire class. Whatever you choose to play, make a plan to keep downtime to a minimum. Keep your students actively involved throughout by making the game as visual as possible, by enlarging the game board, and keeping points on the chalkboard. Allow teams to brainstorm an answer rather than having just one student answer the question, and give all teams an opportunity to answer. You can also create your own games, but keep in mind the previous suggestions, and strive to create a game that emphasizes learning and cooperation—rather than competition—among the teams. To further ensure positive play, remember to review your behavioral expectations and the rules of the game before and during play. Specific games for encouraging and reinforcing appropriate behavior can be found in *Common-Sense Classroom Management for Middle and High School Teachers* (Lindberg, Evans Kelley, & Swick, 2005).

▶ 2. Independent silent reading time is considered a reward by many students, especially if you allow them to read materials of their choice, such as romance novels, the sports section of the newspaper, or a teen magazine. But be sure you check the materials brought in by your students to ensure that they are appropriate.

▶ 3. Quiet conversation time can also prove to be a very motivating reward. Allow your students to earn minutes during the class hour—five minutes or so—that they can cash in at the end of the hour for quiet conversation, desk games such as tic-tac-toe, hangman, cards, independent reading, or computer time. Or instead of doling out a few minutes at the end of each class hour, you and your students may opt to bank time to earn a longer free time on a specified day. If you decide to use this option, it's critical to plan activities from which students can choose. This doesn't mean everyone must do the same thing—just that all students know what is permissible during their free time.

▶ 4. It might be surprising to discover that the opportunity to have lunch with you might be a highly motivating reinforcer as well as a great opportunity to forge a connection with hard-to-reach students. Because you are working with teenagers, you will most likely want to eat lunch together someplace other than the cafeteria as your students may feel self-conscious surrounded by peers. A better option is to make arrangement to meet for lunch either in your classroom or other area of the school. However, do make it a public place to avoid the appearance of impropriety. Lunch with you doesn't need to be fancy or costly. Have the student get his or her lunch from the cafeteria while you supply dessert; or if you want to make it a special event, serve pizza, submarine sandwiches, or fast food.

▶ 5. While we're on the subject of food as an incentive, you can reward your entire class for appropriate behavior by having a party. Food could include pizza, soda, popcorn, doughnuts for a breakfast party—or even a build-your-own sundae party. You might want to do a bit of research before you pick up the tab for this reward. For once-in-a-while events like this, an administrator might be willing to help defray the cost, especially if it's for a good cause, and you ask him or her to drop in. Also, check with your administrator and other colleagues to find out if your school has a partnership with a local restaurant. Many fast-food establishments have certificates they donate to schools to be used as rewards for just such occasions. Finally, you may want to make the event potluck, and ask students to contribute. For instance, you could supply the ice cream while students volunteer to bring in the toppings and bowls.

Backup Plans for Students Not Earning the Incentive

Whole-class rewards and incentive programs are great for encouraging teamwork. But wait a minute, you say, what do I do with those students—and there are always a few—who didn't earn the reward? Here are some teacher-tested ideas.

▶ 1. Although many of the previous suggestions are meant to reward the entire class, there are usually a few students who are chronic and consistent abusers of your rules. You can't continually punish the entire class for the actions of a few. So, keep a brief log of the infractions of those who abuse the rules so they know why they are being excluded. Also consider excluding students who have not completed their homework or class assignments. If your rewards and incentives are enticing enough, you may eventually be able to minimize the number of nonparticipants when they see what they are missing.

▶ 2. You may have colleagues on your teaching team with whom you've already made arrangements to exchange students for a cooling off period when needed. If so, ask whether they would take the students who didn't earn the incentive into their classroom during reward time. Of course, be sure to send class work or a silent reading book so the students will be of minimum bother. Then, be ready and willing to reciprocate when your fellow teacher needs your assistance. You may decide within your teaching team to coordinate a whole-class reward or incentive program for the entire unit. If so, each of you can take a turn hosting the reward event while the other(s) sits with those who cannot attend.

▶ 3. Just as with providing a continuum of incentives, you may also want to provide a continuum of removal. If you would like a student to complete missing work during the reward time or to behave appropriately while under another teacher's supervision, give him or her an incentive. Let the student know he or she has a chance to earn some time toward the reward by either completing assignments or sitting quietly and cooperatively for a specific period of time.

▶ 4. What if you are unable to make arrangements with another teacher to take students who have not earned the reward? See if you can arrange for an aide to supervise your students elsewhere. If that's not an option, arrange the room so only the students who can participate in the reward are able to see the movie and have access to the treats. Sometimes, especially with younger middle school students, being in the same room where all the fun is happening can be more miserable than being removed. One last suggestion is to offer the reward during your or your students' lunch hour. Invite only those who have earned the party in your classroom.

Consequences

No one likes to be the bad guy, particularly when dealing with students with disabilities who often have a number of obstacles to overcome. But realizing that there are consequences for inappropriate actions is a lesson everyone must

learn, and we do a disservice to our students if we don't teach that lesson. Read on for ways to do this in a fair and compassionate way.

▶   1. Because negative consequences are punitive in nature, they should be used sparingly and only after positive consequences have proved ineffective. Negativity is like a snowball at the top of a hill: give it a push, and it will continue to grow bigger and more out of control as it rolls downward. Similarly, when a negative consequence is given to students, chances are they will respond in kind. If you keep these consequences rolling, you will begin to notice that over a short period of time the entire climate of your classroom takes on a negative tone. Kind words become less frequent, work production decreases, and students stop coming to class. If this sounds familiar, reassess your current classroom management techniques, and work toward regaining a more positive environment. Remember, classroom management based on negativity is never successful.

▶   2. Despite all your efforts to employ positive classroom management techniques, there will be times you will have to administer a negative consequence. Put some serious thought into the kinds of negative consequences you choose to include in your classroom management repertoire. Make sure they are logical and that they fit the crime. For example, a logical consequence for an assignment not submitted would be to complete it in the classroom after school. An illogical consequence for this infraction would be a written punishment. Because the severity of the consequence should parallel the severity of the infraction, you may want to develop a graduated menu of consequences. For instance, the first time a student talks to a peer during instruction, administer a verbal warning. The second time it happens, direct the student to a different desk, and the third time, send that student to a colleague's classroom to complete the assigned work.

▶   3. Students need to realize that there are positive as well as negative consequences for their actions that are ultimately determined by their behavior. Consider holding a classroom meeting to generate a list of positive and negative consequences for adhering to classroom rules. Figure 4.3 is an example of something you may want to use. Consider posting these alongside your classroom rules.

▶   4. Consequences should not be a surprise. It's not enough to post them and trust that your students will remember. You need to include them as you give a warning. For example, rather than given a nonspecific warning such as, "Eric, stop talking," be more specific and say, "Eric, if you continue talking to Lisa you will be asked to move to another desk." By letting students know what will happen if they continue the behavior, the likelihood of an argument when the next level of consequence is administered is decreased.

When You Must Discipline

Your method of disciplining a student can often have a direct effect on your success. Above all, remember that you are the adult and should stay in control of yourself—difficult as that can be at times. Look below for some other things to consider.

Figure 4.3 Classroom Consequences

Positive Consequences	Negative Consequences
• Positive call home	• Negative call home
• Incentives, rewards, treats, prizes, coupons	• Forfeiture of incentives, rewards, treats, etc.
• Praise	• Redirection/correction
• Self-control	• Teacher control
• Privileges	• Loss of privileges
• Independence	

▶ 1. One of the most important things a teacher can remember about dealing with challenging students is to treat them with as much respect and dignity as possible. The reality is that often tempers flare and confrontations occur. But remember, you are the adult. Stay as calm as possible. Yelling or shouting is ineffective. If you feel too upset or angry, arrange a time when you can talk more rationally to the student. Often a problem need not be settled immediately. You may feel too flustered to make an appropriate decision about a consequence, and as a result may assign something you cannot implement. If this happens often enough, you will lose credibility with your students.

▶ 2. Afford the misbehaving student the courtesy of speaking quietly and calmly to him or her and, whenever possible, out of view of the rest of the class. A quiet, calm approach away from prying eyes may go a long way to calm a student and convince him or her to back away from inappropriate behavior.

▶ 3. Pick your battles. Is it worth a confrontation to make a student with challenging behavior pick up a piece of paper off the floor? Probably not. Is it necessary to stop that same student from repeatedly knocking things off another student's desk? Yes. Save face for yourself and the student by making a wise decision about potential confrontations.

▶ 4. Don't back a student into a corner in a discipline situation. Offer some choices to resolve the problem. This allows the student to see it as a way for him or her to make the decision rather than having you, the teacher, make it. Often, that's really what a confrontation is about—who has the power—and you've given some to the student in an appropriate way. Then, allow the student some downtime. He or she may need a little time or space to cool off and reintegrate into the classroom without further embarrassment. If the student comes back into the room mumbling under his or her breath—bite your tongue. The student is either trying to re-engage the battle or is just blowing off steam. Either way, if you ignore the behavior, it will more than likely stop after a minute or so. However, if you take the bait, be ready—the bell for round two has just rung.

▶ 5. Don't peg a student as a problem in your eyes because he or she will quickly gain a reputation throughout the building—perhaps unfairly. Do your best to treat all your students alike. Even though you need to discipline or confront challenging students more often than others, try hard not to let those feelings color the rest of your interactions with him or her that day. This sends the message that you are unhappy with the behavior, not the student. Find something you genuinely like about that student, and concentrate your efforts on helping him or her develop that attribute. This may take time and patience, but it could help smooth the way for improved behavior.

Functional Behavioral Assessment and Behavior Intervention Plan

The situation is very serious with one of your students, and a formal behavior plan is required. Don't let this job responsibility stress you out. Developing and implementing a realistic BIP really depends on common sense and a good understanding of your student. With these thoughts in mind, read on, and relax.

This strategy provides an overview of the FBA/BIP process. Two Web sites for additional information on conducting an FBA and developing a BIP are the Center for Effective Collaboration and Practice (http://cecp.air.org) and the Online Academy (http://www.onlineacademy.org/). Please familiarize yourself with your district procedures as well as changes in the new IDEIA that may affect you as a teacher by accessing your state and district Web sites.

▶ 1. A Functional Behavioral Assessment (FBA) is a formal approach to dealing with problematic behavior. The purpose of the FBA is to determine the underlying motivation behind particular behaviors. The Behavior Intervention Plan (BIP) is a highly individualized course of action developed to support the student in learning more appropriate behaviors. The interventions and strategies developed for the BIP are based on the findings of the FBA.

▶ 2. School districts around the country develop their own formats for FBAs and BIPs. For this reason, this strategy will not discuss specifics, but be sure you understand the details of the format used by your district. There are, however, some generalities that will most likely apply to your situation. For instance, FBA and BIPs are typically completed for students who have ongoing or escalating challenging behavior that has been resistant to change, are engaging in potentially dangerous behaviors, or who have committed a serious offense. Be sure you know what infractions in your school district constitute a serious offense. In addition, federal law states that an FBA and BIP must be created for students who lack access to their IEP due to removal because of misbehavior from their educational setting for more than 10 cumulative days in a school year. Removal from the educational setting not only includes suspension from school, but also removals from the placement designated on the IEP without continued instruction on IEP goals. For instance, removal could include time spent in a detention or in-school suspension room or being sent to an administrator's office. Check with your district to see which situations deny access to the student's educational program. Also see Chapter 7 for more detailed information about FBAs and BIPs.

▶ 3. As the special education teacher, you will most likely be responsible for initiating the FBA. Keep track of behavior infractions and consequences administered, and particularly suspensions issued, to the student. Be mindful of the 10-day removal regulation mandated by federal law. Because the FBA/BIP process requires an IEP meeting, the parent or guardians must be invited as well as other school professionals who would attend an annual review of the IEP.

▶ 4. The BIP is a plan of action that should enable you to replace the target inappropriate behavior with a more acceptable behavior. Data collected from the FBA are used to develop the BIP, as the function of the behavior must be understood before an appropriate intervention can be put in place. For example, if the results of the FBA suggest that a student is engaging in an inappropriate behavior to avoid a difficult assignment, the BIP would provide the student with a more acceptable behavior to avoid the work as well as build in supports to enable the student to practice the new behavior. But wait a minute, you say, why would we want to allow the student to avoid work? That's not an acceptable behavior. Actually, most of us have engaged in some sort of avoidance behavior when faced with a challenging task. For instance, we might put off completing a project or take a short break from a task when we begin to feel frustrated. Most likely, your student isn't using one of these more appropriate choices. Your job is to teach the student one of these strategies or another more acceptable alternative.

▶ 5. The terminology used to describe the FBA/BIP process can be quite confusing. Following is a glossary of commonly used terms.
   a. *Target behavior*—This is a succinct, observable, and measurable statement of the problem behavior.
   b. *Function of behavior*—Behavior serves a purpose and tends to fall into one of three categories: to get something, to avoid something, or to communicate something.
   c. *Antecedent or trigger*—These are factors that tend to provoke the target behavior.
   d. *Consequence*—These are events that immediately or promptly occur as a result of the behavior. Consequences can either maintain or encourage the recurrence of the behavior or extinguish or decrease the likelihood of the behavior being repeated.
   e. *Preventive strategies*—These are strategies built into the BIP with the intent of decreasing the likelihood of the target behavior occurring.
   f. *Replacement behavior*—This is a more appropriate alternative behavior taught to the student that will replace and serve the same function as the target behavior.

Conducting a Functional Behavioral Assessment

Sometimes a student's behavior becomes so serious that informal behavior programs don't work, and something more formal and intensive is required.

Don't be afraid to tackle an FBA. If done correctly and thoughtfully, it should provide what is needed to write a BIP that will be successful.

▶ 1. The first step in conducting an FBA is to identify a target behavior. As a team, develop a concrete description of the behavior to be addressed. The target behavior should clearly describe what the behavior looks or sounds like and should not include assumptions regarding the motivation behind or triggers for the behavior unless there is clear evidence to support these assumptions.

▶ 2. Once a target behavior is identified, the team should determine whether sufficient data regarding the behavior have been collected. Because the data will be used to develop a hypothesis regarding the function of the student's behavior, you will want to have a considerable amount of varied data available for analysis. To help make this determination, consider the following questions:

   a. Have a variety of types of data collection such as questionnaires, observations, interviews, or records been used? Because the student may engage in the behavior for any number of reasons, a single source of data will most likely not provide sufficient insight into the function of behavior.

   b. Does the data come from various individuals such as teachers, the student, parents, or other involved staff? The student may behave differently with different individuals for any number of reasons, such as compatibility, subject content, time of day, and so on. Also, tolerance for and perception of behavior varies from individual to individual. Compiling data from varied individuals may decrease the influence of personal bias as well as provide information regarding settings in which the behavior tends to occur or not occur.

   c. Is there baseline data on the present level of occurrence? For instance, is there concrete data regarding how often the behavior occurs or how long the behavioral episode tends to last? To monitor the effectiveness of the behavior intervention plan, baseline data must be noted. Other concerns related to baseline data include the settings in which the behavior tends to occur, including the time of day, specific locations such as subject area classrooms, hallways, and so on, and who tends to be present?

   d. Do the data provide sufficient information on antecedents and consequences that may influence, provoke, or reinforce the target behavior? For instance, is the team able to identify common triggers, such as requests to complete class work that is too difficult, boredom, and so forth, that tend to precede the occurrence of the target behavior? In addition to looking for patterns in antecedents, the team should also review the data for similarities in the consequences issued for the behavior.

▶ 3. If the team determines there is insufficient data on the behavior to move forward, they must decide which additional information must be collected, the types of data collection instruments to use, for how long data will be collected, and who will assist in gathering the data. As previously noted, to increase validity, it is best to use multiple sources of data to gather information across several different settings and from a variety of individuals. Because different types of data collection will provide different information, be mindful of selecting methods that will provide answers to specific questions about the student's behavior. Following are three types of data collection methods, as well as recommendations for use.

    a. *Event recording*—The purpose of this type of data collection is to determine the frequency of a behavior. It will be most accurate for behaviors that have a discrete beginning and end, such as shouting out answers or getting out of one's seat. Tally marks on a piece of paper are typically used to note the occurrence of the behavior. In addition to the total number of occurrences, also record the date, setting, and starting and ending time of the observation period.

    b. *Duration recording*—This type of data collection is used to determine how long the student engages in a behavior. Duration recording could be useful in gathering information on the number of minutes a student wanders around the room, or engages in a tantrum or other behaviors. In this instance, the goal of the BIP would be to decrease the length of time the student engages in the behavior. Record the onset and cessation of the behavioral event as well as the date and setting of the observation period.

    c. *Interviews*—Although interviews do not produce baseline data, they are useful for creating insight into where, with whom, when, and possible reasons why a student engages in a particular behavior. Several individuals should be interviewed, including the student and perhaps the parent.

▶   4. After the data have been collected, another IEP meeting is held. The data are analyzed, and the team develops a hypothesis regarding the function of the behavior. Once the team has come to consensus on the function of the behavior, the next step is to develop a BIP.

Developing a Behavior Intervention Plan

If an FBA is carefully and thoughtfully completed, it should enable you to develop a BIP that can provide you with a successful way to eliminate—or at least greatly minimize—inappropriate behavior. Look below for some solid advice on how to make this happen.

▶   1. As with the meeting held during the FBA phase, the development of the BIP is also an IEP team meeting. Because the purpose of this meeting is to develop a plan to support the student and encourage more appropriate behavior, the student should also participate in the meeting. It goes without saying that because other staff members will be involved in implementing the BIP, it is unwise to develop it without input from them. As you think about the components of the plan and discuss it with your colleagues, the most important thing to remember is that the plan must be realistic. Don't create anything that either you or other staff involved cannot actually implement. Remember that if a behavior is so serious that there is a need for a BIP, a workable plan must be created.

▶   2. Remember that the BIP is created to support the student during the process of learning a more acceptable behavior. Support may take the form of alterations to the environment, changes in the instruction or curriculum, or other interventions put into place to prevent or decrease the likelihood of the student engaging in the target behavior. These interventions should be proactive rather than reactive and should focus on positive rather than negative consequences.

► 3. During the FBA, a hypothesis regarding the function of the student's behavior should have been determined. This information is critical to developing an appropriate BIP, especially as the team identifies a replacement behavior that the student can use instead of the target behavior. Thoughtful consideration should go into determining a replacement behavior. Keep in mind that the target behavior has met a particular need for the student, so the replacement behavior must also meet this need, or the student will see no value in using it. Begin by asking the student to suggest an alternative behavior with which he or she would feel comfortable. Then talk about devising an incentive plan discussed earlier in the chapter to add additional encouragement. Finally, when devising a replacement behavior, make sure you are not asking the student to do something that he or she is incapable of doing. For instance, it may be unrealistic to expect a student with a regulatory disorder such as Attention Deficit Hyperactivity Disorder to remain in his or her seat the entire class period. If the function of the student's behavior is to expend energy, a more appropriate replacement behavior should be chosen. For example, give the student permission throughout the class hour to move about for productive reasons, such as helping to pass out journals, erase the chalkboard, and so forth. Also, remember to consider the student's strengths and how these can be supported in the plan.

► 4. Once a replacement behavior has been determined, the team should develop a plan for providing instruction in using the replacement behavior. Opportunities for direct instruction, practice, and review should be built into the plan. To further strengthen the learning process, the team should also generate a list of positive consequences to offer the student in recognition of using the replacement behavior. Also, develop a list of negative consequences to administer in the event the student continues to engage in the target behavior.

► 5. Finally, refer back to baseline data and establish a criterion for success. Identify periodic times to review the effectiveness of the plan. The success of the intervention depends on monitoring and ongoing evaluation. Remember also that very few interventions last forever, so anticipate that a new one may need to be considered at some point.

5 sits at the top right.

General Education Instructional Planning

Students with disabilities have the right to access the general education curriculum. In fact, federal law mandates that students with disabilities be provided access to the general education curriculum as well as the opportunity to receive their education within the general education classroom to the greatest extent their disability allows. It's primarily the job of the special education teacher to provide that access. However, you can't do it alone. Collaboration between special and general educators is a crucial factor in enabling students with disabilities to gain the most from their involvement in the general education classroom. Read on for suggestions for how you and your general education colleagues can work together to provide quality access to the general education curriculum.

Chapter Outline

- Your Involvement in the General Education Classroom
- Planning for Academic Success
- Planning for Behavioral Success
- Grading Students With Disabilities
- Coteaching and Co-planning

Your Involvement in the General Education Classroom

Do you feel like persona non grata in the general education classroom? Regardless of the number of classrooms in which you support students, you can become an important contributor to the education of all students. Here's how you can accomplish this important goal.

▶ 1. It is extremely important that the general education teacher is aware of his or her responsibilities in implementing the Individualized Education Program (IEP). Be sure each teacher is aware of pertinent IEP goals for all students with disabilities. Plan a time, if possible, to review these with the teacher, and address questions and concerns. The section "Sharing Student Information" in Chapter 3 provides insight into what information should be shared.

▶ 2. The amount of direct special education services required per the IEP and the number of classrooms in which you must support students will dictate your level of involvement within the classroom. For instance, you will be able to take on a much more active role if you work in one classroom the entire period versus a schedule in which you must travel across several classrooms within one class hour. If students have not already been placed, you may want to propose a schedule to your administration. See "Providing Educational Services" in Chapter 3 for suggestions on creating schedules. Be an advocate for appropriate services for your students. If students are spread out over too many classrooms, consider realigning schedules to include more students within fewer classrooms per class hour, thereby allowing you the opportunity to provide additional direct support to each class. If it's too late for the current semester, check whether changes can be made for the following semester or make a note to do so for next year.

▶ 3. You will need to meet with all the general education teachers to plan your involvement in each classroom. Ideally, you should be able to do this during regularly scheduled department or unit meetings. However, if you don't have common planning time, take the initiative to meet with your general education colleagues, preferably as a teaching unit so you can all be on the same page. Ask for weekly lesson plans, and together decide in which classes it is most critical that you provide support. (See Figure 1.2 in Chapter 1 for a weekly lesson plan form.) Depending on the activities in each of the classrooms, your schedule and level of involvement may change from week to week. For instance, on Monday you may lead teach a whole-class math review, while on Tuesday you might provide one-on-one assistance to a student with a disability during the test. These are decisions best made by both you and the general education teachers in a way that will benefit all the students and be mutually comfortable for the teachers.

▶ 4. Take an active role in the classroom regardless of the amount of time you are there during the class period. If you sit back and wait to be needed, not only do you run the risk of students not recognizing you as a teacher in charge, but you may also garner resentment from general educators who may feel that you are not carrying your share of the load. More important, you are there to help the students with disabilities access the general education curriculum. Because many students do not want one-on-one assistance as they fear it may call attention to their disability, it may be more beneficial to provide support through other means. Following are just a few suggestions for how you can support students with disabilities by taking an active role in the lesson.

    a. Lend visual support to students by writing notes on the board or on an overhead projector as the general educator lectures. Depending on the needs of individual students, you may also want to provide students a copy of these notes after class.

    b. Demonstrate an activity. For instance, demonstrate the steps of a science experiment, for completing a math problem, and so forth. Students who do not comprehend written or auditory directions will appreciate the opportunity to *see* what they need to do.

    c. During large group instruction or independent work time, circulate around the room to check students' work, monitor on-task behavior, answer quick questions, or make on-the-spot academic adaptations. Because you are working with all students in the classroom, you are less likely to red flag the student with a disability.

    d. Take on the role of lead teacher by assigning and leading a discussion on a journal prompt, playing a review game with the class, or even teaching the entire class learning strategies for taking notes, preparing for a test, and so forth. By providing instruction to the entire class, you are able not only to support the students with disabilities, but to also lessen the likelihood of singling out students with a disability.

▶ 5. Although you should have an active role in the classroom, be careful not to bite off more than you can chew. For instance, some special educators attempt to team-teach with every teacher with whom they work every class hour of the day. This can prove a daunting, if not impossible, task as it would require considerable planning time with each teacher as well as time to prepare for each lesson. Before you overbook, take a few minutes to review your responsibilities for the week. Note the students to whom you must provide additional support and the specific classrooms in which you need to spend time for whatever reason. Once you have your week mapped out, create a realistic plan for how active a role you can play in the classes in which you will be working. For example, many teachers find it feasible to team-teach with one or two teachers per school day, and then assume a less active role in the remainder of classes as noted in number 4 of this strategy. Although the level of coteaching used should be dictated by the needs of the students with a disability, try to vary the types of coteaching used in each class so that all teachers and students in your unit can reap the benefits of teachers working together. You can find additional information on coteaching later in this chapter in the section "Coteaching and Co-planning."

Planning for Academic Success

General and special educators need to work together to help students with disabilities gain the maximum benefit from the general education classroom setting. Plan to meet with the general educators working with your students before the semester begins and bring along a copy of the students' IEPs to

ensure individual student needs will be addressed. Read on for additional suggestions for how you and your general education counterparts can work together to help students with disabilities reach their academic potential.

▶ 1. Find out what instructional methods the general education teacher plans to use. Compare these techniques with the students' abilities as identified on their IEPs. Determine whether additional academic supports will be needed to help students or whether only minimal changes need to be made. For instance, if the teacher plans to use a lecture format for many lessons, one student may require a complete set of notes to follow along, whereas another student may only need an outline highlighting key points written on the board.

▶ 2. Despite minor changes to instruction, students with disabilities frequently require specific academic adaptations, known as accommodations or modifications, to succeed. These terms are often confusing to both general and special educators alike. The following information can help you and your general education colleagues speak the same language.

    a. "Adaptation" is a broad term that covers changes of any kind that are made to general education to help students with disabilities learn. There are two kinds of adaptations—accommodations and modifications.

    b. Accommodations are minor adjustments to instruction or materials that help students with lesser disabilities access the curriculum without changing the content, expectations, or activities. One example of an accommodation is to allow a student who works at a slower pace additional time to complete an assignment. A second example would be to allow a student with a writing disability the opportunity to dictate his or her answers to a scribe. Because many accommodations are acceptable for use during standardized testing as well as at the postsecondary level, students should feel comfortable in using them, so you will want to include them as day-to-day supports as well. For a complete list of allowable testing accommodations, check with your state's Department of Instruction or Education. If the student is planning to attend college or another postsecondary institution, contact the establishment to find out what accommodations are allowed as well as the procedures for accessing services.

    c. Modifications, on the other hand, are significant changes to the general education curriculum that impact the content, expectations, or activities. For instance, a student with a significantly lower academic ability level may be allowed to write a one-sentence response to a question while the rest of the class is expected to compose a complete paragraph. Another example of a modification to written assignment requirements would be to grade an essay solely on content and not on the mechanics of writing, such as grammar and punctuation. An example of a modification in the area of math would be to assign a student to add fractions while the rest of the class is working on multiplication of fractions. Note that because modifications change the outcome, they are not allowed during standardized testing and may also impact credit earned within a general education classroom.

▶ 3. When determining adaptations, strive to select those that allow the student to do the work with a minimum of frustration yet still challenge the student to learn a new skill. Be aware of how much and what kind of adaptations your students need. For example, don't assume that a student who has difficulty finishing a full page of adding decimals doesn't understand how to add. For whatever reason, he or she may simply need a more limited number of problems to solve or perhaps extra time to complete the work. Either of these minor accommodations may address the student's needs without overaccommodating. Also, pay attention to when a student may no longer need an adaptation. Your student's math confidence may build, and soon he or she may be able to complete an entire page.

▶   4.   If your students are in a general education setting for all or most of their academic instruction, it would be ideal to have access to lesson plans so you know what is ahead for them. For various reasons, however, this may not always be possible. If lesson plans are unavailable to you, another way to obtain information is to provide the general education teacher with a form on which to indicate upcoming academic lessons. (See Figure 1.2 in Chapter 1 for an example of such a form.) You can provide the most assistance to your students by being up-to-date on what they are learning, and it is important for you to make every effort to get this information.

▶   5.   If you are able to access lesson information ahead of time, you will have more opportunity to make suggestions, adapt tasks, or provide alternative assignments. Usually, most general educators feel comfortable with providing accommodations. Special education teachers, however, will more than likely be responsible for making modifications, such as creating a different assignment or an alternative format for a worksheet or test. Be open, however, to any suggestions or ideas general educators may have about how to help students with disabilities succeed. Because these teachers have probably had much more extensive training in the content area, they may be able to provide very practical and helpful strategies.

Planning for Behavioral Success

Teaching students with challenging behavior is one of the concerns most often cited by general educators. These teachers often feel ill-prepared to address the behavioral needs of students with disabilities and worry about the effect a student's disruptive behavior can have on other students' learning and the overall classroom climate. As the special education teacher, you will want to devise a plan to support both the student with a behavioral challenge and the general educators teaching that student. Ideally, you will be able to provide direct support within the general education classroom; however, there may be class hours in which your schedule does not allow for this. A plan of action that can be implemented with or without you will increase the likelihood of successful inclusion for the student with behavioral challenges.

▶   1.   Boynton and Boynton (2005) identified three times of day when students are most likely to be off task or become disruptive. According to the authors, the greatest number of behavioral incidents occur as students enter the classroom, during transition times within the class hour, and during the last two minutes of class. With this information in mind, talk with your general education teachers to assess current practices and determine if additional proactive strategies may be needed to decrease the likelihood of behavior problems during any of these times. For instance, a daily opening assignment, such as review problems or a journal prompt, could help students settle in at the beginning of the class hour. Or taking a moment to remind students of behavioral expectations prior to changing from one activity to the next might help to decrease the chaos that typically ensues.

▶   2.   If you are including a student with a behavioral challenge in the general education classroom, build in as many opportunities for success as possible. For instance, consider the student's academic skills and, if need be, make sure appropriate academic adaptations are in place so the student doesn't fall behind or act out due to frustration. Or, if you are working with a student who has a tendency to become disruptive when angered, devise a plan with the student and your colleagues in which the student is able to take a short break to cool off.

▶   3.   Sometimes students with behavioral disabilities do not know how to behave appropriately because they are unsure what appropriate behavior is in certain situations. If this is the case, identify, with the student and general educator, a classmate who all of you believe is a good role model. Direct the student with the behavioral disability to defer to this person when unsure about how to act. For instance, if the student isn't sure whether to laugh at the behavior of a peer, he or she could take a quick look at the role model to see how that person is behaving. Another idea is to establish a buddy whom the student can talk to when unsure what to do. Use either of these strategies carefully, not only to respect the confidentiality of the student with the disability but also to ensure that an appropriate classmate role model or buddy is identified.

▶   4.   Many general educators use a classroom management program. Their program may or may not provide a sufficient level of support for the student with a behavioral challenge. Before you suggest a more individualized plan for a particular student, consider whether the established plan requires only a few minor adjustments to be more effective. For instance, if the teacher tends to use generalized compliments such as "nice job class," perhaps he or she could incorporate a nonverbal cue to privately signal the student that his or her appropriate behavior has been duly noted. Another minor adjustment could be to seat the student in an area where the teacher frequently stands or walks. Then the student could easily be redirected or reinforced as the teacher moves about the room.

▶   5.   The special education teacher will be responsible for devising a more individualized behavior management plan if a student with challenging behavior requires one. However, because general educators will have to implement it, be sure to include them in its development. Although the plan should specifically address the needs of the student, one that is practical and can be easily incorporated into the classroom will increase the likelihood of success. Once a plan has been developed, review it with your general education colleagues every few weeks to decide whether it's still working or if it needs revamping. Your willingness to address behavior problems and to follow through on revising the plan if needed will let your general educators know that you are a team player.

Grading Students With Disabilities

There are several aspects to grading students with disabilities that should be discussed with your general education colleagues. Be forewarned that this may be one of the more intense conversations you will have with the general educators. Before you begin this discussion, check to see whether your school district has established guidelines for evaluating students with disabilities. If teachers have leeway in grading students with disabilities, set aside time to meet with your colleagues to determine which grading and assessment methods will be used. Following are some things to consider when grading students with disabilities.

▶ 1. In addition to district mandates, your school may have its own policies on grading. For instance, in the upper grades—and probably more so at the high school level—policy may dictate that because the student with a disability is included in the general education classroom and earning credit for the course, he or she will be held to the same performance expectations as peers who are nondisabled. In these instances, accommodations are provided as "access ramps" to the content, although a consistent grading criterion is used for all students. For example, a student with a writing disability would be required to answer the same comprehension questions as other students but would be allowed to dictate answers to a scribe or record the answers rather than submitting written responses. Although this grading policy maintains the integrity of the course content for all, some students with disabilities may feel frustrated because their grade may not reflect the amount of effort they put into the work. Because of this, both parents and students should be made aware of this grading policy.

▶ 2. Regardless of the grading policy in effect, you and your general education colleagues should review planned assessment methods and grading procedures to make sure that they measure the student's learning and not his or her disability. For instance, the handwritten responses of a student with a fine motor disability will more likely reflect the student's challenges than knowledge. Minor changes, however, could be made to assignments and test formats to provide a more accurate depiction of learning. For instance, rather than expect all students to write a book report, teachers may give students the option to write, draw a comic strip, or orally present their report. Tests that require students to match terms to definitions can easily be reformatted to accommodate students with reading challenges by simply placing the definitions on the left side of the page and the terms on the right. By using this format, the amount of rereading required to determine the correct answer is decreased while expectations for mastery remain the same. See Figure 5.1 for an example of how to reformat a test.

▶ 3. Make sure that both adaptations to assessment and grading are fair to all students. Adaptations to assignments should provide the student access to the content and the opportunity to demonstrate his or her learning; they should not give the student with a disability an unfair edge over his or her peers in the general education setting. As classrooms become increasingly more diverse, general educators have begun to incorporate elements of Differentiated Instruction or Universal Design for Learning into their teaching and evaluation of learning.

Figure 5.1 Alternative Test Format

A. The science of studying plants and how to grow them.	1. Boll weevil _____
B. A beetle that infests cotton plants	2. Botany _____

These teaching philosophies recognize the unique learning needs of all students and allow for flexibility in assessment as well as other areas of teaching and learning. You can learn more about Universal Design for Learning by visiting the Center of Applied Special Technology Web site at http://cast.org/index.html. A good resource on Differentiated Instruction is: *The Differentiated Classroom: Responding to the Needs of All Learners* by Carol Tomlinson (1999) and published by the Association for Supervision and Curriculum Development.

▶ 4. For students with disabilities who require additional adaptations to be successful in the general education curriculum, there are several adaptations to tests that can be made. The following information was adapted from Friend and Bursuck (2006) and Vasa (1981).

a. A number of strategies can be used prior to testing to help students with disabilities. For instance, teach students how to prepare a study guide or another type of learning strategy to help them organize and recall information. Another strategy is to administer a practice test to help students learn *how* to take the test. You may also want to consider whether the test format should to be altered. For instance, additional white space may eliminate visual clutter or provide more space to write for a student with fine motor difficulties. Adaptations can also be made during testing. For instance, the student may be given additional time to complete the test, may take the test in a different classroom, or may be allowed to use an assistive technology device to record answers.

b. Alternative grading techniques may also be used for some students with disabilities. Keep in mind that changes in grading procedures must be documented within the IEP. Also modified grades may impact a student's official enrollment in the general education classroom, and as a result the student may not receive credit for the class. To clarify, although the student may be participating in the general education curriculum, he or she is being evaluated differently from peers who are nondisabled because the student is working on a different curriculum than the rest of the class. There are several alternative ways to grade students with disabilities. Following are some for your consideration.

- Points can be given for assignments, with a total number of points designated for an A, B, C, and so on.
- Shared grading in which teachers decide on the grade—the percentage depending on the adaptations that must be made to the general curriculum.
- A contract may be made to allow the student to complete certain parts of an assignment for a specific grade. For example, to earn an A, the student must complete the entire assignment (possibly with adaptations).

To earn a B, the student may omit one part; and to earn a C grade, the student could choose to do a more limited part of the assignment.

- IEP grading is a way to measure the student's competency levels on the basis of his or her IEP goals and objectives. For example, if the IEP notes 85 percent accuracy as the goal criterion, you could develop a modified grading scale in which a score of 85 percent would equate to an A.
- A multiple grading system is one in which the student is evaluated on several different criteria, such as ability, effort, and achievement. For example, a student could receive 20 points for completing the assignment on time, 40 points for including all sections of the project, and 40 points for using five or more resources.

Coteaching and Co-planning

Coteaching can be one of the most effective instructional techniques for supporting students with disabilities within the general education classroom as well as a means for ensuring that a "highly qualified teacher" is teaching students with disabilities. Good coteaching relationships, however, rarely happen without skills in collaboration and communication. Following are several considerations for creating an effective coteaching program.

▶ 1. Several factors will determine whether you are able to coteach: the needs of your students, the model used in your school for providing services to students with disabilities, and your schedule will all affect your level of involvement within the general education classroom. If you will be sharing teaching responsibilities by coteaching, there may be times when you must be creative. For instance, depending on the type of coteaching used, you may have to prepare a lesson to teach to the entire class while keeping foremost in your mind the needs of your students with disabilities. Although there may be times when one of you must take on a greater percentage of the work, there are some things that you can do to make coteaching work for you, your colleague, and most important, the students.

    a. If at all possible, plan to meet with the general education teacher before you begin to coteach. Take a few minutes to get to know each other's teaching styles, expectations for behavior, and feelings about working with another teacher. The more issues you can bring to the forefront prior to teaching together, the less chance problems will arise.

    b. In addition to planning to coteach, you will also want to establish regular lesson planning time. Many teachers find time to meet during a common preparation hour. If that isn't an option, you may need to be creative. Perhaps your schedule can be tweaked to allow for 10 to 15 minutes of common planning time each day. Another option is to create planning time during the class hour by taking a few minutes during independent student work time to prepare for the next day's lesson.

    c. During planning time, make sure to address lesson objectives, procedures for teaching the lesson including the type of coteaching that will be used, adaptations for specific students, and how learning will be assessed.

d. If face-to-face planning time is impossible, consider alternatives such as sending lesson plans via e-mail, jotting notes to each other in a notebook, or using a lesson plan book specifically designed for coteaching teams, such as the *Co-Teaching Lesson Plan Book: Academic Year Version,* by Lisa Dieker (2002).

e. Regardless of whether you use a prepared document, a notebook, or even a traditional lesson plan form, co-planning is crucial. One suggestion for planning when unable to meet would be for the general education teacher to jot down lesson specifics and pass them on to the special educator. The special educator would then add adaptations for certain students, make a copy of the lesson plan for reference, and return the original to the general educator. As a means of further clarifying roles, each teacher should initial or highlight the parts of the lesson for which he or she will be responsible before passing it on to the other.

▶ 2. There are several different ways in which teachers may choose to coteach. The type of coteaching selected will be determined by factors such as the needs of the students, subject content, teacher schedules, and the teachers' comfort and experience with coteaching. Following are some of the most common types of coteaching and specific considerations for each. (Information about the types of coteaching is from Friend and Cook (2003)).

a. *Lead teacher; support teacher*—This is often one of the most commonly used types of coteaching as it requires the least amount of planning time. With this particular model, one teacher, usually the general educator, assumes lead responsibility for teaching the content while the other teacher, usually the special educator, circulates around the room to answer individual questions, records notes on the chalkboard, or monitors classroom behavior.

b. *Station teaching*—With this type of coteaching, teachers share in instruction by dividing the lesson content. Each teacher takes responsibility for preparing and teaching a portion of the lesson to one-half of the class. During the planning stage, teachers decide if they will switch groups to allow all students to receive the same content or if each station will deliver instruction targeting different skills. An example of the second option would be one teacher providing instruction on creative writing while the other teacher reviews the mechanics of writing.

c. *Alternative teaching*—This type of coteaching is generally composed of whole-class instruction in content led by the general educator and additional support provided to specific students via small-group work, usually led by the special educator. This small-group support may include preteaching or reteaching a skill or providing an opportunity for those students who understand the skill being taught to engage in enrichment activities.

d. *Parallel teaching*—With this type of coteaching, teachers co-plan a lesson, and then each delivers instruction of the same content to one-half of the class. Even though the content is the same, teachers often elect to use different modes of instruction as a means of providing more individualized support. For instance, one teacher may use manipulatives during instruction of how to balance equations while the other teacher may choose to use paper and pencil activities.

e. *Team teaching*—With this type of coteaching, teachers take on an equal role in preparing and providing instruction to all students. Because teachers need to collaborate during both the planning stage and throughout instruction, this type requires more planning than other types of coteaching. Despite this added responsibility, both students and teachers often benefit from the expertise each teacher brings to the relationship.

▶ 3. Although coteaching will afford the opportunity to provide direct services to your students with disabilities, you will want to continually assess whether you are sufficiently meeting their educational needs. Talk with your coteacher to find out what role he or she plans to take in supporting the students. Decide whether you can build adaptations into lessons or if you will need to supplement instruction with adapted work. In addition to academic considerations, decide how you both will manage behavior problems during instruction. Talk about each of your roles and responsibilities in disciplining students, contacting parents, and implementing individualized behavioral plans.

▶ 4. Collaborate with your general education colleague on what type of ongoing evaluation you will use for students with disabilities. It is best not to wait until report card time to decide how you will grade your students. Keep written records of grades as well as some work samples as evidence. Ongoing evaluation with input from general education teachers will make report card time much less stressful as you will have a solid basis for the grades you assign.

▶ 5. Looking for more information about coteaching? Here are a few excellent resources:
   a. R. Villa, J. Thousand, and A. Nevin, *A Guide to Co-Teaching: Practical Tips for Facilitating Student Learning* (Thousand Oaks, CA: Corwin Press, 2004).
   b. The Northern Nevada Writing Project Teacher-Research Group, *Team Teaching* (Portland, ME: Stenohouse Publishers, 1996).
   c. M. Friend and L. Cook, *Interactions: Collaboration Skills for School Professionals* (4th ed.) (New York: Allyn & Bacon, 2002).

6

Specially Designed Instruction

One of the most important aspects of teaching for the special educator is instructional planning for the unique needs of your students. Depending on your students, you may provide not only academic instruction, but also instruction in appropriate school behaviors, life skills, self-advocacy, transition, and so much more. Providing instruction to students with different needs who may be working at a variety of skill levels can challenge even the most systematic and knowledgeable teacher. This chapter can help you organize your lessons to address Individualized Education Program (IEP) goals and to maximize achievement for your students.

Chapter Outline

- Implementing the IEP
- Finding Appropriate Materials
- Individualized Work
- The IEP and Assistive Technology
- Using Assistive Technology as a Learning Support
- Learning Strategies
- Transition Planning
- Transition Planning for Students Bound for Postsecondary Education
- Instruction in Behavior

Implementing the IEP

A student's IEP is a legal document that must be addressed throughout the school year and should be kept foremost in your mind as you plan your lessons. Academic programs for students with disabilities should be based on that student's IEP goals. Here are some tips for keeping this important document in the forefront of your planning.

▶ 1. If you are teaching in a resource setting, you will have more control over your planning and your ability to directly address IEP goals and objectives. But if you are working with your students in an inclusive general education setting, you will need to teach with and plan with the general education teachers. General educators should be working in tandem with you to implement the IEP goals of the students with disabilities. It will be up to you as the special education teacher to find a way to ensure that this happens. Ask your colleagues to meet with you periodically to review the IEP to make sure progress is being made on goals and objectives. Keeping abreast of your mutual students' growth will reap benefits for both of you at conference and report card time and also when you are preparing a student's annual IEP review.

▶ 2. An IEP snapshot can be a helpful tool for communicating IEP goals with others as well as providing a quick reference for you. This should be a simple form that contains the most important information on the IEP, such as goals and objectives (if applicable), testing information, brief notes on behavior, present level of performance, and related services. You may also want to include space to write brief progress notes on the IEP snapshot. Use the format in Chapter 1, Figure 1.1, or create one of your own, but be sure to include this important information. Because general educators also need to implement the IEPs, be sure you give every general education teacher working with the student a copy of the IEP snapshots. Don't forget about others working with the student such as fine arts teachers, vocational educators, and paraprofessionals who will also need a copy.

▶ 3. Develop a formal method of keeping track of progress made toward IEP goals and objectives. Remember that your planning must be aimed at helping your students with disabilities meet these goals. Don't depend on your memory to keep track of each student's progress. Brief, daily notes in a notebook or in your planner are easy ways to document. Also, if you are using daily or weekly reports with your students, you could file these as documentation of progress.

▶ 4. Remember that planning should consider two important things: the IEP goals and objectives (if applicable) of your students, and what is being taught in the general education classroom. Even though the ability level of your students may be lower than their grade level, your lessons should reflect an effort to connect with the general education curriculum. For example, if students in the general education classroom are reading about the Civil War, find some books on this topic at the ability level of your students for the basis of your lesson. If the math lesson in the general education classroom is about multiplying decimals, and your student doesn't know multiplication facts, allow him or her to use a multiplication chart when practicing the process. Do be cautious when using lower-level resources that the materials look age-appropriate. Bunnies and kittens on a primary math sheet may help an elementary school student learn how to count, but they are inappropriate for an older student. Finally, don't forget the documentation you are keeping to show the progress your students are making on their IEP goals.

▶ 5. By law, each state has developed a set of academic standards. These standards are the objectives in each academic area toward which general classroom educators direct their teaching. Because students with disabilities are expected to meet these standards as well, you will want to align your teaching as much as possible to the general education curriculum. If students fail to make adequate yearly progress (AYP) in reading and math, their schools could face a variety of remedial measures including school closure. This accountability measure creates an even greater impetus than IDEIA to link special education IEP goals to the content standards of the general education curriculum. (The information about AYP can be found at the National Association of School Psychologists: http://nasponline.org.)

Finding Appropriate Materials

Finding and selecting teaching materials can sometimes be a frustrating task for special education teachers, who may need to scramble for leftover textbooks and other resources. To add to the frustration, age appropriate materials for older students working at significantly lower ability levels may not be easy to locate. Keep in mind that you are the advocate for your students with disabilities, who have the same right to access the general education curriculum and materials as their counterparts in general education. Look below for some ways to ensure your students have what they need.

▶ 1. If you are new in your school and have few materials or none at all, do some investigating to find out how you can get the general education curriculum materials you need. Some schools have storage rooms where extra books are kept; other teachers may have extra copies of texts and teachers' manuals; some schools have math or reading support persons, content area department chairs, or other staff who often know how to access these materials. Some school districts have centers that loan out a variety of curriculum materials to teachers much as a library would. Find out what applies to your situation. If none of these are applicable to you, you may need to go to your principal or the special education administrator in your building. Remember that you are not asking for yourself but rather are advocating for your students, who are entitled to the same learning experiences as their counterparts in general education.

▶ 2. Whether you are working in an inclusive general education classroom or special education classroom, you will most likely need to do some lesson adapting for your students. Some of your students may only need accommodations—small changes that will help them get the same results as the students in general education. However, for other students, you will have to modify work to their skill level or provide alternative materials. Students who are reading considerably below grade level may need alternative reading materials, and there are good resources for these types of books. (See number 5 in this strategy for a list of Web sites of publishers who provide these kinds of materials.) Again, do some investigating to determine whether your school has some of these things. The librarian might know, or other special education teachers could have them.

▶ 3. Veteran general and special education teachers are good resources for materials. Find these friendly, welcoming people—there are always some in every school—and ask if they have ideas or materials they would be willing to share with you. But, remember that if you borrow something, be sure to return it—and in the same condition as you received it. Then reciprocate when you can by offering an idea or lending them some useful materials. Another key person could be the school librarian. That person might even be willing to purchase resource materials for you if the library budget permits.

▶ 4. Remember that as you plan your lessons using modified materials, high-interest, low-skill-level books, or other appropriate resources, you should be coordinating your lessons with what is being taught in the general education classroom. Do your best to work with the general education teachers so you know which materials are being used and whether you can access them for you students if you feel it is appropriate. That said, the reality is that it may not always be possible to make this connection, but do so whenever you can.

▶ 5. Another good resource for materials for students with disabilities is, of course, teaching supply stores—and you don't always have to bring your wallet. If you have a little time and paper and pencil, you can browse around and jot down ideas that you find in books. You can also look for academic-related posters that might work for your students, record what you see, and make your own. There are even some academic games that can provide ideas. In addition, catalogues can be a source for ideas about curriculum and supplementary materials. Check your school library or the faculty room or other designated area for this type of information. Sometimes teachers have catalogues they use frequently that they can recommend or lend to you. Before getting out your own checkbook or credit card to pay for these materials, check with your administrator to determine whether funds are available, as some of these books and other resources can be costly. Look online to find publishers who offer high-interest, low-skill-level books. Below is a list of some:

> http://www.donjohnston.com: Provides intervention materials in reading, word study, and more

> http://www.capstonepress.com: Nonfiction and social studies books for readers from grades 3–9

> http://www.wieser-ed.com: High-interest, lower-reading-level books, including career education and life skills math and reading for students functioning below grade level

> http://www.perfectionlearning.com: Age-appropriate learning materials for students working below grade level

Individualized Work

When we think of teachers, we often picture them standing in front of the room, providing instruction to the entire class. This may not be the case for you, as in any given class hour you could have students working at significantly different skill levels, different rates, or even doing work for entirely different content areas. Following are suggestions to help you be successful with this juggling act.

▶ 1. If you are working with a very diverse group of learners, you may find it more practical to develop individualized work packets. Work packets not only allow students to work on their IEP goals but will also free up time for you to provide direct instruction to one or a few students who need additional support. Keep in mind though, that individualized work should be something that students can complete more or less on their own—but it shouldn't be just busy work.

▶ 2. It is highly likely that you may have students coming and going from the special education setting as they work on different skills and needs. Although you will want the students to settle in and get to work promptly, you may not have an opportunity to meet with each to get them started. One solution is to provide each student with an assignment folder. To use this strategy, staple to the inside of the folder a form for recording assignments such as the one provided in Figure 6.1. Then, prior to class, write the daily assignment on the form, and place any worksheets inside the folder. As students arrive to class, instruct them to review their folder and complete the next assignment. At the end of class, ask students to place their work inside the folder. When students finish the assignment, they should record the date with their initials next to it—this lets you know that the work is ready to be graded. To let students know that you have received their work, write your initials on the form. Then use the comments box to let the students know the grade earned, what corrections are needed, if any, or any positive feedback you may have for them.

▶ 3. Even if your students are completing individualized work, this doesn't mean that they must work entirely independently. For instance, you may want to coordinate the assignments of two or three students so that they can work together or work with you. In fact, you should regularly attempt to build in time to meet with each of your students. This may include providing direct instruction prior to completing an assignment or periodic checks to assess learning or productivity. To indicate to the student that he or she must meet with you, place a mark such as a star, small ink stamp, or "see me" sticker next to the assignment noted on the form. However, try to avoid overbooking yourself by staggering your appointments.

▶ 4. If you have students who are frequently absent or who produce the minimum amount of work, use the assignment form to develop a work contract with them. For instance, if there are 30 school days during the mark period, the contract may state that the student will earn a C if he or she submits 20 assignments with a score of 75 percent or better, a B for 35 assignments at 75 percent accuracy, and so forth. Then, number the lines of the assignment form to help the

Figure 6.1 Assignments

Name _____   Mark Period _____

1. Please complete the next assignment on the list. When you have finished the assignment, place it in your folder. Record the date you finished the assignment and your initials on the assignment sheet.

2. Look at the assignment sheet and make corrections to assignments that do not have teacher initials.

Assignment	Date completed	Your initials	Teacher initials	Comments

students keep track of how many they have successfully completed. A strategy such as this helps students realize that they control the outcome, and if carefully thought through with criteria for success that are achievable, the student will feel a real sense of accomplishment.

▶ 5. If you are not the teacher grading the student's work, you will want to find some way in which the students will earn credit or at least some sort of incentive for assignments completed with you. Without this, the work can become purposeless for the students. Talk to the teacher who is grading the student and ask whether work completed with you can count toward the student's grade. Or, develop an incentive program in which the students can earn computer time, consumable items, or some other motivating reinforcer.

The IEP and Assistive Technology

The use of assistive technology within the IEP can sometimes be confusing for teachers. But keep in mind that this issue must be addressed for students who need it to demonstrate academic understanding. Most schools have a variety of personnel who can assist you with deciding how to include assistive technology appropriately in the IEP. Read on for help with this and other questions.

▶ 1. The IDEIA legislation defines assistive technology as a device or a service. The term "assistive technology device" means any equipment—whether it is sold commercially or it is something modified or customized—that will increase, maintain, or improve the skills of students with disabilities. The term "assistive technology service" means any service that directly assists a child with a disability in the selection, acquisition, or use of an assistive technology device. Assistive technology supports services in many areas including writing, reading, math, study skills, communication, positioning and mobility, hearing, vision, recreation, and leisure.

▶ 2. The need for assistive technology devices or services must be considered for each student with a disability. There may be a difference between the need for a device or service to benefit the student versus the need for the device or service to enable the student to demonstrate knowledge, so make sure you are aware of exactly how your school district interprets this. If you have any questions about this, be sure to check with the special education administration in your building.

▶ 3. Assistive technology is included in the IEP as accommodations and modifications. Be aware that these areas may overlap and can include such things as computers, note-taking devices, software, large print, and audio-taped materials. The overlap can sometimes be unclear. Again, be sure to consult with the special education administration if you are confused about where a certain device or service should be addressed.

▶ 4. Be sure to check with the special education administration in your building before you indicate any specific type of assistive technology, such as the brand name of any piece of equipment. If you specify a brand name, be aware that any school the student might attend would need to purchase that specific piece of apparatus—and it could be very costly. Using a generic term such as talking word processor rather than a brand name gives the school more choices. No one wants to deny students with disabilities the access to appropriate assistive technology, but budget constraints exist in almost every school system and must be considered.

▶   5.   Know the people in your building who can be resources in the area of assistive technology. They can include the speech and language therapist, the physical and occupational therapist, and your school's general technology person. This person may deal mainly with computers but could be an excellent resource for software programs that could be very beneficial for students with disabilities. Also, most school districts have technology personnel who often provide workshops to help keep teachers up-to-date on the latest resources. Often, a districtwide technology department will send out newsletters that may include, among other things, information about these workshops. Find out how you can access this, and take advantage of what the department has to offer.

Using Assistive Technology as a Learning Support

Some of us are intimidated by technology and its speed of change. However, not only do we owe it to our students to keep up with the many new devices that are available to help them learn, but we are mandated by law to provide these services when required. So plunge in, and learn about these wonderful learning aids.

▶   1.   Assistive technology can be helpful to a broad range of students, not just those who have severe physical or cognitive disabilities. Assistive technology is a means for students with varying levels of ability to access the curriculum and to aid in independent learning. As you assess your students with disabilities, think about whether and how some of these resources could be used.

▶   2.   Keep in mind that there are both low-level and high-level technology options. Something as simple as a pencil grip for a student who has difficulty with fine motor skills is low-level technology. Clearly this kind is less intricate, less costly, and requires little or no training. Other low-level technology devices could include such things as highlighters for text, large print books, special paper, book holders, and picture-word communication boards. As noted in the previous strategy, the line between low-level technology and accommodations or modifications can be blurry. If you need to include any of these items in an IEP and are unsure how to document them, check with someone from the special education administration in your school.

▶   3.   High-level technology can be more complex and might require training to use. As noted in the previous strategy, most school districts have technology departments that offer workshops on using these high-tech devices. Some of these departments might also lend these technologies to schools for a specified time. This can give teachers an opportunity to try the device with the student to determine whether it will be useful without having to purchase it first. Be sure to investigate what your assistive technology department has to offer and take full advantage of any opportunities.

▶ 4. As noted previously, the speech and language therapist and the occupational and physical therapists are also good resources for ideas for technology devices or services. Don't hesitate to ask for their help and suggestions. Given that they are right on the premises, they might be willing to come into your classroom and help you assess a student, offer some technology ideas, and even show you how to implement the technology.

Learning Strategies

Learning strategies are all the little tricks we use to help us remember information. For instance, most of us remember the colors of the spectrum by recalling the mnemonic ROY G. BIV, and we remember telephone numbers or our social security number by chunking the individual numbers into small groups. The ability to store and quickly retrieve information is not just a party trick but a skill we can use throughout our lives. Continue reading to find out how you can help your students become more successful players in the game of life.

▶ 1. Learning strategies are cognitive strategies that enable students to become independent learners. The intent of a learning strategy is not only to help the student recall information but also to provide strategies for acquiring, storing, and organizing incoming information. Examples of learning strategies include graphic organizers, study guides, and mnemonic devices.

▶ 2. One of the most commonly used learning strategies is a mnemonic device. Mnemonic devices include acronyms, phrases, jingles, rhymes, poems, and pictorial images. ROY G. BIV is an example of a mnemonic device created by taking the first letters of each word: red, orange, yellow, and so forth. Another similar type of mnemonic is to create a phrase by using the first letter of each word. For instance, students may remember the correct order for completing mathematical operations by learning the following: "Please Excuse My Dear Aunt Sally." In this phrase, each letter corresponds to the first letter of the mathematical operation (parentheses, exponents, multiplication, division, addition, subtraction). Search the word mnemonic on the Internet and you will find hundreds more mnemonic devices to choose from.

▶ 3. Study guides and note-taking templates are also learning strategies that help students become independent. However, bear in mind that in addition to teaching the students how to take notes, you may also have to teach the students how to use their notes. For instance, you may have to teach students how to locate key words or think about what the questions are asking. For the student who needs visual support, teach him or her how to create a graphic organizer as a means to "see" the connections.

▶ 4. Many students with disabilities will require guided instruction on learning and applying the strategies. As the teacher, you will want to not only teach the steps and procedures for the strategy, but also teach the student how to assess the situation and decide on an appropriate strategy to use. For instance, if you are working with a student who had difficulty recalling the steps in a process, you may teach the student to use a sequence map. Instruction in this learning strategy does not simply consist of telling the student that he or she should put things in order. It also consists of teaching the student how to generalize the strategy to other situations. If you may have initially taught the student this learning strategy as a means of remembering the steps in a math process, then he or she should be able to recognize this strategy as helpful for remembering how to work a combination lock, travel from one classroom to the next, or follow a recipe. Another component to instruction in learning strategies is teaching the student how to analyze content to determine relevant and irrelevant points. To clarify, imagine this student uses the sequence map strategy to make chocolate chip cookies and is following the recipe on the bag of brown sugar. Relevant information would be all the ingredients as well as the sequential order for mixing and baking. Irrelevant information would be the brand name noted on the bag of brown sugar—another brand would most likely be a comparable substitute.

▶ 5. As mentioned above, many students with disabilities will require guided instruction in learning strategies. The Learning Toolbox Web site (http://coe .jmu.edu/LearningToolbox/) is an excellent site that provides step-by-step instruction for teaching learning strategies as well as several different learning strategies for skills such as organization, math computation, editing written language, and test taking. In addition to providing information to teachers, the site is also designed for use by parents and students.

Transition Planning

We all have dreams and ambitions. However, some of us require additional guidance and support in achieving them. Transition planning is not only a legal requirement but also a great way to help students with disabilities reach their goals.

▶ 1. Transition services can start as early as the upper elementary grades but, per IDEIA, must take place no later that the first IEP in which the student will turn 16 years old. Please be advised that your state or district may mandate that transition services begin at an earlier age. Regardless of when you begin addressing transition, you and other members of the IEP team—including the student—will first identify the student's postsecondary plans. Then the team will develop a plan of action that includes course work, life skills, study skills, and so forth, all of which are needed to prepare the student for life beyond high school.

▶ 2. Think about what you wanted to be when you grew up. It's probably safe to say that you had more than one career in mind and that not all your ambitions were entirely grounded in reality. Chances are that at least some of your students are thinking the same way. As teachers, we should play an important role in helping them make an informed decision about their future. When your student is considering unrealistic career choices, help that student to investigate the prerequisites for these jobs. This activity might provide him or her with the insight to make more realistic choices.

▶ 3. Students often make their career decisions on the basis of professions with which they are familiar. For instance, the latest TV shows often make an impression on young people, who may then want to consider a profession they see portrayed. Help the student find out exactly what it is about the job that most interests him or her. Then, on the basis of the response, provide a list (or teach the student how to investigate this) of several other jobs with similar requirements. This will help the student to decide whether it is the job itself or some aspect of the job that is attractive.

▶ 4. One of the most important skills you can teach your students related to successful transition is that of self-advocacy. Quite often, students with disabilities are uncomfortable with communicating their specific needs and asking for assistance. To help your students become strong self-advocates, work with them to identify areas of strength as well as areas in which they need adaptations. Talk about what type of information is appropriate to disclose and to whom they may need to disclose it—future employers, university faculty, and so on—and build in opportunities to practice self-advocacy. This practice could include having the student tell his or her teachers about necessary adaptations, completing and distributing their own IEP snapshot, or running their own IEP meeting. There are many good Web sites that provide easy-to-understand, accurate information about transition planning. Some of them are listed below and not only will they help you feel more comfortable with writing transition plans, but they are great resources to share with parents and students.

Schwab Learning: www.schwablearning.org
National Center for Learning Disabilities: www.ncld.org
National Center on Secondary Education and Transition: http://ncset.org

Transition Planning for Students Bound for Postsecondary Education

Many students with disabilities hope to go on to college or trade school following high school. The reality is, however, that too often their postsecondary educational experience doesn't turn out as planned. Continue reading for valuable information on how you can help increase the potential for a successful educational experience.

▶ 1. Many students with disabilities never get the chance to enroll in a postsecondary educational setting because they did not take the high school courses required for entrance into college. As you work with them—regardless of their present age—ask if they are intending to go to college or trade school. If the answer is yes, help the student and the parents investigate course work requirements for a few different institutions in the area. This will not only assist in developing a transition plan, but will also give the student and family an opportunity to begin thinking about the most appropriate postsecondary school.

▶ 2. It is important that you, the student, and parents are familiar with the differences in allowable accommodations at the postsecondary level. Adaptations to allow access to general education and to provide the opportunity for academic success are provided under IDEIA. However, once a student with a disability leaves high school, IDEIA entitlements cease and now fall under the Americans with Disabilities Act (ADA). Under the ADA, accommodations at the postsecondary level are only provided to allow access, thus significantly decreasing the number of permissible accommodations. Information on allowable accommodations can often be found on the postsecondary institute's Web site.

▶ 3. Most postsecondary education settings require documentation of the student's disability. This is typically a copy of the formal testing results conducted as part of initial diagnosis. However, this varies from school to school so you, the student, or the parent will want to investigate requirements for schools in which the student is interested. As the IEP teacher, you may have to assist the family in getting this documentation or ask that the student be reassessed, as some post-secondary sites require the results of recent evaluation. In addition to testing results, another document that the student can provide to the postsecondary institution is a newly mandated document per IDEIA called a Summary of Performance (SOP). This document affords the student written information to share not only with postsecondary institutions, but also with future employers, or if necessary, independent living centers. The SOP is completed during the student's last year in high school and should include a summary of the student's academic achievement, functional performance, and recommendations for how to assist the student in meeting postsecondary goals.

▶ 4. To receive accommodations, the student must provide appropriate documentation of disability to the department in charge of serving students with disabilities. Common names for this department are the Student Access Center or Disability Support Office. Documentation may include the results of formal testing or SOP. Once the department receives the documentation, it will be reviewed. If the student is determined eligible for services, the department will provide the student with a letter detailing needed accommodations that the student must give to each faculty member.

▶ 5. As you help prepare your students for transitioning to a postsecondary institution, keep in mind that in addition to the Disability Support Center, most schools also offer other services that may benefit the student. For instance, many schools provide tutoring services for a nominal fee and offer workshops on such topics as writing skills, using a computer, or even time management. Encourage the student and his or her family to explore these services or offer to assist by researching the school Web site with the student.

Instruction in Behavior

As mentioned in Chapter 3, schools must offer a continuum of service delivery options to meet the needs of students with a disability. If your job assignment is to teach students who demonstrate significant inappropriate behaviors, you will need to teach your students more acceptable behavior in addition to academics. Not sure you have the background and training to do this? The following suggestions should help ease your mind.

▶ 1. Know that students with behavior disabilities might behave as they do because they cannot behave differently due to a medical, physical, or mental health condition or because they have learned over time that their inappropriate behavior more effectively meets their needs than a more socially appropriate one. Keep this in mind as you develop instructional strategies to teach behavior and when determining both negative and positive consequences. This will help you maintain consistency in your approach and to ensure that you are not punishing a student for actions beyond his or her control.

▶ 2. Teach behavior as you would an academic skill, through guided instruction, practice, and encouragement. Following are a few suggestions:

    a. Your lesson plans should not only include academic objectives but behavioral expectations as well. For instance, if you are planning to have students work with a peer to complete an assignment, think about what working together will look like and sound like. Will you want to see equal contribution to completing the task? Will both students need to read and write, or will they divide the responsibilities? Do you expect students to talk quietly such that others will not be distracted? Do you want to hear on-task conversation and the use of constructive feedback rather than criticism? When it's time to teach, write the behavioral expectations on the board, and introduce them along with the academic objectives for the lesson.

    b. Reinforce and redirect behavior throughout instruction by using specific comments related to your behavioral expectations. Whenever possible, try to recognize the more appropriate behavior rather than the negative one. For instance, rather than saying "Alex, stop talking. Others are still working on the test," a more instructive comment would be to find a different student demonstrating the appropriate choice. Then point that out by saying something like "Sarah, good idea to read a book at your desk while others are finishing up on the test." A comment such as this not only cues students on how they should behave, but also provides no reinforcement to the student who may be engaging in an inappropriate behavior to gain attention. If you want to avoid singling out particular students, an alternative is to use a blanket statement such as, "Thanks to all of you who have found something quiet to do at your desk like reading or drawing while others are still completing the test. Remember, consideration for others is a sign of maturity."

    c. Another way in which you can provide ongoing feedback to your students regarding their behavior is to award bonus points periodically throughout the lesson to all students who are meeting the behavioral expectations. You can easily do this by using a marker or some a uniquely colored pen—a color other than one that students use. Place a tally mark at the top of each student's assignment, or if students are working on a group project, record the point on an index card. The bonus points are then added to the final grade for the assignment. If a student earned 15 points on the assignment and 5 bonus points during the class hour, he or she would have earned a total score of 20 points. Points can also be awarded during whole-group instruction, by giving students credit for participating in the lesson. These points should be recorded in your grade book and ultimately be averaged into the final grade.

    d. Don't dismiss the effectiveness of doling out primary reinforcers, such as small snacks or tokens every once in a while. Most of us are quite familiar with their power. For instance, we may reward ourselves with a special treat or purchase following the completion of a difficult or unpleasant task. Businesses often provide bonuses in the form of money, gift certificates, or other consumables to employees who meet a set quota. If you are particularly pleased with how well your group of students is working, distribute small candy bars or a small bag of a salty snack to let them know that you appreciate their efforts.

e. Whenever possible, give students a chance to correct their behavior before issuing a negative consequence. It's rather unfair to punish them without having given proper warning or reminding them of what they should be doing—and students will often call you on this. To avoid the possibility of an argument following the administration of a consequence, warn students ahead of time when they are pushing the limits, and remind them of the possible consequence. For example, "Robert, if you continue talking to Anne you will be asked to move to another desk."

▶ 3. Instruction on appropriate behavior should be included in every class hour. This doesn't mean that you must spend an inordinate amount of time discussing behavior or providing direct instruction on controlling one's anger. With clever planning, you can infuse mini behavior lessons into just about any lesson or activity. For instance, journal prompts for Language Arts class or review questions following a history lesson could provide students an opportunity to reflect on behavior or consequences of actions. Or create discussion questions for a novel the students are reading, and include a few questions to get the students thinking and talking about the event, the actions of the people or characters, and the motivation behind their behavior. You may be able to use them to translate into a discussion about issues with which may be affecting your students. For instance, if your class is reading the novel *Maniac Magee* by J. Spinelli, you may pose a question such as: "The Beale family treated Maniac Magee very well, why do you think he ran away from their home?" Or if your students are learning about the Amistad in history class, post the following prompt: "The word 'amistad' in Spanish means 'friendship.' Do you think *Amistad* was a good name for the ship that sailed with the Mende African slaves? Answer yes or no and be prepared to support your answer."

▶ 4. You can also practice classroom rules and expectations by playing group games such as bingo, hangman, 20 questions, and team games. Begin by posting and explaining behavioral expectations. Let students know that they must meet these expectations in order to play and, furthermore, that you will not accept their responses if they don't follow them. You may also want to let students know that bonus points will be periodically awarded to those teams or individuals demonstrating sportsmanlike conduct. In addition to group games, board games such as chess or checkers or card games can also be used for practicing appropriate social skills.

▶ 5. There are many good resources available to help you teach behaviors such as social skills, self-esteem, conflict resolution, and so much more. Following are some resources you may want to consider:

ESR Resources for Empowering Children: Conflict Resolution Lessons for Middle and High School Students. Available at: http://www.esrnational.org/MidHigh.html

B. Johns, E. Crowley, and E. Guetzloe, *Effective Curriculum for Students With Emotional and Behavioral Disorders* (Denver, CO: Love Publishing, 2002).

D. Mannix, *Social Skills Activities for Secondary Students With Special Needs* (San Francisco: Jossey-Bass, 1998).

G. Rogers, *The Seven C's of Thinking Clearly* (Midvale, UT: Choice Skills, n.d.).

7

Legal Issues

The legal responsibilities for a special education teacher can be daunting, and in many districts the paperwork addressing these legal issues is complex and changes from year to year. Since each school district and each state has their own method of interpreting how some of these issues should be addressed, this chapter will not discuss specifics. But read on for helpful ideas that generally apply.

Chapter Outline

- Changes to the IEP Process as Required by IDEIA

- Transition

- Student and Parent Rights

- Transfer of Rights

- Functional Behavioral Assessments and Behavior Intervention Plan

- Manifestation Determination

Changes to the IEP Process as Required by IDEIA

The Education for the Handicapped Act of 1975 (PL 94-142) was the first federal legislation that set guidelines for special education services. Despite several reauthorizations over the years, the basic principles of PL 94-142 have remained relatively intact. IDEIA is the latest revision in legislation. Following are some of the key provisions of IDEIA. (Please note that state requirements for Individualized Education Programs (IEPs) may vary, so please be sure you are aware of your district and state requirements.)

The information regarding changes to the IEP per IDEIA came from the State of Wisconsin Department of Public Instruction. The Web address is http://www.dpi.state.wi.us.

▶ 1. An IEP review meeting must be held annually. However, revisions, or minor changes to the IEP may take place throughout the school year for reasons such as the student reaching an IEP goal or perhaps adding an additional accommodation. Historically, these revisions to the IEP were completed through an IEP team meeting. IDEIA provides greater flexibility for parents and schools by allowing them to make minor changes to a child IEP without reconvening the IEP team. To do so, however, all IEP team members must agree to this and a written document noting the changes must be created. Again, be sure you know your district's policy on implementing this procedure.

▶ 2. Per IDEIA, there are two circumstances where IEP team participants may not need to attend an IEP team meeting. First, a staff member can be excused from attending if that person's area of the curriculum or related service is not being addressed at the meeting. Second, a staff member may be excused if that person has submitted information about the student in writing prior to the meeting. Be advised, however, that the parents or guardian must agree to this option in writing.

▶ 3. Historically, IEPs were required to address annual goals and short-term objectives (benchmarks) for all students with disabilities. IDEIA states that short-term objectives can be eliminated for all but a small group of students who take alternative assessments based on alternative achievement standards. Be sure to check with your school district to see whether it plans to implement this directive.

▶ 4. Since IDEA 1997, IEPs must include a statement on how the student's progress toward annual goals would be measured and the method for informing the student's parents on progress toward the annual goals. Per IDEIA, in addition to this information, the IEP must also note *when* periodic reports on progress will be provided.

▶ 5. Under IDEA 1997, IEP teams began to address transition when the student turned 14. Per IDEIA, the transition process begins at age 16 and is considered an outcome-based process more than just a plan. See the next section for more information.

Transition

Transition planning first became a requirement of the IEP under IDEA 1997. Several new requirements have been included in IDEIA in an effort to strengthen transition planning. Read on for the most current, need-to-know information regarding transition planning.

(Information for this strategy comes from: www.schwablearning.org and the National Center for Learning Disabilities: www.ncld.org.)

► 1. Per IDEIA, transition must be addressed "beginning no later than the first IEP to be in effect when the child is 16." This does not mean that transition planning cannot start at an earlier age—in fact most experts recommend that planning for postsecondary transition begin at a much earlier age.

► 2. Requirements for planning for transition include:
   a. Appropriate, measurable postsecondary goals based on age-appropriate transition assessments related to training, education, employment, and, if needed, independent learning skills.
   b. Transition services based on the student's strengths, preferences, and interests.
   c. A statement of transition services related to the student's postsecondary goals, including courses of study necessary for reaching these goals.

► 3. Planning for transition is conducted as part of an IEP team meeting. As the goal of transition planning is to help the student prepare for life beyond high school, the student must be an active participant in this transition planning. Parent input is also highly recommended. Other people who may be invited to the IEP meeting include representatives from outside agencies such as the Department of Vocational Rehabilitation Services (DVR) or others who can provide information specific to the student's goals and needs (community services, college support services, and so forth).

► 4. The transition plan should be reviewed at least annually (during the annual IEP meeting) to make sure that the student's needs or interests haven't changed, to measure progress toward goals, and to ensure course work requirements are being fulfilled.

Student and Parent Rights

All students and their parents or guardians have rights within a school system. It is very important that all teachers are aware of what these rights are and that they understand them. Although these rights will differ from district to district across the country, the information below provides some examples of what might be included. Be sure you know your district's policy.

► 1. It is important for all teachers to know which family members have the legal right to access school information—or the legal right may belong to a guardian. Court-appointed guardians must provide documentation to the school indicating their rights in relation to the child. Legal guardians can attend IEP meetings and make school-related decisions for the student.

► 2. Most school districts provide parents or guardians with student handbooks and may also have a policy and procedure manual. Individual schools within the district may also have their own handbooks. Be sure to know what your school district provides, and obtain a copy of each. Read them over, and familiarize yourself with anything that could pertain to your students. Note that many of the rules and regulations that affect students in the general education classroom also affect those with special education needs.

▶ 3. Parents should be the best advocates for their children. Below are some parent rights that are common to most school districts.

    a. The right to review their child's school records and to receive copies of information in the school records

    b. The right to expect that records and information about their child will be kept confidential

    c. The right to receive academic and attendance reports for their child

    d. The right to request conferences with teachers or administrators to review progress reports and attendance, disciplinary actions, tests, and so forth

    e. The right to visit the school and their child's classroom

    f. The right to have an interpreter if they are hearing impaired or if they do not speak English

▶ 4. All parents or guardians, or adult-aged students, have the right to due process if they have a complaint or concern. Ideally, the first step should be to try working with the teacher and school principal, as most concerns can often be resolved this way. If the person with the complaint is not satisfied with the outcome at the school level, he or she can contact a parent advocate. Many school districts have a parent information center that can provide this service.

▶ 5. In addition to those afforded all students, students with disabilities have additional rights. Some of the rights of parents or guardians of children with special needs include the following:

    a. To request and receive copies of individual IEP reports to review before the IEP meeting

    b. To be advised of procedural options by the IEP team if a concern is not addressed at the meeting

    c. To bring an advocate to an IEP meeting who can help parents or guardians understand their rights, explain procedures, and raise questions and concerns

Transfer of Rights

Because students with disabilities can receive special education services until the age of 22, you may find yourself teaching students who have reached the legal age of majority and are thus considered adults. Following is information regarding some of the legal requirements when working with this particular population of students.

▶ 1. Per IDEIA, each state has the authority to determine policy regarding the transfer of rights from parent to student upon the student reaching the age of majority. Age of majority is defined as the age established by state law in which a person is considered an adult and therefore has the right to make legal decisions. In most states, the age of majority is 18. However, if you are unsure, please review your state's law.

▶ 2. For most students with a disability, once they reach the age of majority or once the student goes to college, he or she assumes all rights previously granted to the parents. For students whose disability impairs their ability to make informed decisions, the parent can, prior to the student reaching the age of majority, make a formal request to the state to obtain guardianship.

▶ 3. By law, the school district is required to inform the parent and student of the transfer of rights at least one year prior to the student reaching the age of majority. IDEIA requires this statement to be included within the IEP. To avoid having to hold an IEP review meeting solely to provide this notification, as you plan your calendar for IEP meetings for the school year, note the birth dates and ages of your students. If you find that you have students who will be turning 17 during the school year, be sure to address transfer of rights during their annual IEP meeting.

▶ 4. Transfer of rights does not mean that the parent is no longer able to participate in the educational decisions regarding their child. Most parents want to be informed of their child's progress, and you will find that most students with disabilities want their parents to continue their involvement in their education. In most states, parents of adult students will continue to receive phone calls regarding their child's behavior and receive paperwork such as report cards, progress reports, and notification of upcoming IEP meetings or reevaluations. One difference, however, might be that the adult student must give permission (often in writing) for the parent to participate in the IEP meeting. Each state has developed policy regarding the disclosure of confidential information to parents once their child has reached the age of majority per the Family Education Rights and Privacy Act (FERPA). Please check with your school district to ensure you are compliant with your state law.

▶ 5. Parents are often quite anxious regarding transfer of rights and may have many questions—which you might not feel qualified to answer. Two good sources of information for you to check and to recommend to parents are:

SchwabLearning.org: A Parents Guide for Helping Kids with Learning Difficulties: http://www.schwablearning.org/
The National Center on Secondary Education and Transition: www.ncset.org

Functional Behavioral Assessment and Behavior Intervention Plan

Sometimes a student's behavior becomes so serious that informal behavior programs don't work, and something more formal and intensive is needed. Although this might seem to be a time-consuming and tedious task, the end result may be well worth it as a thoroughly completed Functional Behavioral Assessment (FBA) can provide the information needed to develop an effective Behavior Intervention Plan (BIP).

(The information about FBA and BIP is from the Wisconsin Department of Public Instruction: http://dpi.wi.gov/sped. To ensure that you are in compliance with your state policies and procedures, visit your state's department of public education Web site.)

▶ 1. IDEA 1997 introduced the concept of positive behavioral supports (PBS) as a means to address the behavioral concerns of students with disabilities. Two components of PBS are the FBA and the BIP. Information regarding the legalities of conducting an FBA and developing a BIP are detailed below. Specific details regarding the process of completing an FBA and BIP can be found in Chapter 3.

▶ 2. Per federal law, an FBA must be conducted and a BIP developed in the event of the following circumstances:

a. The student has engaged in a serious offense in which a change of placement will be considered. Serious offenses may include possession of drugs or bringing a weapon to school.

b. The student has accumulated disciplinary removals that exceed 10 cumulative school days during a school year. Be advised that a removal from the educational settings does not only mean suspension from school but includes any other instances in which the student has been removed from the placement designated on the IEP and is not provided instruction on IEP goals. For instance, removal could include time spent in a detention or in-school suspension room, being sent to an administrator's office, or being suspended from riding the school bus.

▶ 3. In addition to the instances noted above, an FBA is often conducted and a BIP developed whenever the student's behavior impedes his or her learning or the learning of others.

▶ 4. In the event a student with a disability is removed from his or her learning environment beyond 10 school days per year, provisions must be made to enable the student to access the general education curriculum to the extent noted in the IEP and to work on his or her IEP goals.

▶ 5. Both the FBA and BIP processes are components of an IEP team meeting. As such, the full IEP team is invited to the meeting. In addition to the legal IEP team composition, other staff members who are familiar with the student or have expertise in areas to be addressed during the IEP meeting may also be invited. Also, because the purpose of the FBA and BIP process is to address the behavior of the student, he or she should participate in the meeting to the greatest extent practical. Although others will most likely be involved in gathering data and ultimately implementing the BIP, as the special education teacher, you will most likely be responsible for setting up IEP meetings as well as monitoring the effectiveness of the BIP.

Manifestation Determination

When a student with a disability commits a serious infraction of a school rule, he or she is subject to a procedure different from that of a student in the general education classroom. Be sure you are familiar with this process and who needs to be involved. Below is some basic information that may be helpful. (The information about manifestation determinations is from the State of Wisconsin Department of Public Instruction: http://www.dpi.state.wi.us.)

▶ 1. When a student with special education needs violates a school policy, it is the responsibility of the IEP team to determine if the violation was caused by or had a direct relationship to the student's disability or if it was the direct result of the student's IEP not being implemented.

▶ 2. If the team, including the parents or guardian, determines that either of the two aforementioned situations applies, then the violation is considered to be a manifestation of the child's disability. In this case, the IEP team must proceed with a manifestation determination. The forms to be used for a manifestation determination will vary from district to district, so check with your special education administrator to determine what is needed in your school.

▶ 3. When dealing with students who have chronic and potentially dangerous behavior problems, the best plan is to be proactive—have an FBA and BIP in place. Then when the IEP team convenes for a manifestation determination, the team can review the BIP and modify or change it as necessary. If an FBA and BIP are not in place for the youth, the team must develop and implement one.

▶ 4. If a student has engaged in a serious offense such as possession of an illegal substance or a weapon, a BIP might not be in place as the school could not have predicted the behavior. It could also be possible that a BIP has already been developed, but for a different behavior. In these instances, an FBA of the serious offense should be conducted, and a BIP that addresses this particular behavior should be put into place as soon as is practical.

8

Working With Families

Working with family members is an incredibly important part of any teacher's responsibilities. Even if you are teaching students who have reached the age of majority (18 years in most states), a successful teacher-parent partnership can help provide critical insight into the student and his or her special education needs. Consider the suggestions in this chapter as you work with families.

Please note: If you are working with students who have reached the age of majority, find out your state and district policies on sharing information with parents of adult children.

Chapter Outline

- Before You Contact Families . . .

- Establishing and Maintaining a Positive Relationship

- IEP Meetings

- Parent Conferences

- Documentation

- Assistance From School Support Staff

Before You Contact Families . . .

Sometimes it can be a real challenge for special educators to establish and maintain a positive working relationship with family members. Keep in mind that families of students with disabilities may be wary of contact with anyone from their child's school as it may have been unpleasant and contentious in the past. Your mission—should you decide to accept it—is to change that perception for the sake of your students. Read on for some helpful precontact tips.

▶ 1. At the beginning of the school year, take the time to look carefully through your students' cumulative folders and Individualized Education Programs (IEPs). Be sure you know the names and relationships of family members or guardians, as sometimes students have a different last name from their family members or may be living with relatives other than their parents. If parents are divorced, check to see who has the legal right to make decisions for the child and who can have physical contact with him or her. Also, be sure you know whose name(s) is on the emergency contact card for your students. Finally, if you are working with students who have reached the age of majority, find out whether the parent has legal guardianship. If not, make note of this, and find out district policy regarding right to privacy afforded to adult students.

▶ 2. Put all this information in a notebook that you can have at your fingertips if needed. But remember that this is confidential and should be kept in a private place. When you call families, you can avoid potential embarrassment by having all this necessary information at hand.

▶ 3. Keeping current with phone numbers is very important but is often an ongoing challenge. To ensure that you have the correct information, you may want to call to obtain important numbers in addition to sending a form home for family members to complete. Sometimes there is no phone in the household, and you may want to ask whether there is a neighbor or other family member living nearby. But be sure they are willing to take phone calls, relay information, or get immediate family members to the phone. If you have a work number for a family member, check to be sure that it is permissible for you to call at work, and update this number periodically.

▶ 4. Remember also that home phones can be disconnected and phone numbers may change during the school year. So you might want to check occasionally to see whether any of these things have occurred. Also, ask if there is a certain time that is best to call at home as some people work nights and sleep during the day. Rousing someone from sleep is not a good way to cement a relationship.

Establishing and Maintaining a Positive Relationship

Ongoing communication does not mean calling families three or four times a week to report bad behavior or to complain about a student. Keeping in touch with families in a way that will ensure their cooperation should you need it is one important objective of good communication. Look below for some useful suggestions.

▶ 1. It is very true that your first call to families should be a positive one. Make an effort to contact families by phone to introduce yourself. Do this during the first or second week of school after you have formed an impression of your students and can find something positive to say about each one—even if it's that you are glad to see him or her in school every day. If circumstances make it impossible for you to contact family members by phone—after you have made every reasonable effort—be sure to send something written in a positive tone. Figures 8.1 and 8.2 provide sample letters of introduction to parents of students with a disability who are included in a general education setting. Then, once you've made the initial contact, don't be a stranger—keep the communication going throughout the school year. And remember that parents are anxious to hear positive things, so don't forget how important it is to call, or write, with good news.

▶ 2. During one of your earlier contacts, ask family members if their child has any special circumstances you need to know about. For instance, a student might be in therapy, under the care of a medical doctor, or living with someone other than a parent. Family members may also share that there is a divorce happening or that there has been a death in the family. If the student is receiving therapy, ask the parents or guardian for permission to share information with the therapist. Help family members to understand the importance of being able to work with the therapist to assist with positive progress for their child at school. Most likely, you will need a release of information form that your administrator or support staff can provide. This will allow you to discuss the student with the therapist on an ongoing basis. Information about things happening outside of school can provide clues to behavior at school. If family members choose not to share information, respect their right to privacy. However, if you suspect there may be something occurring outside of school that is affecting the student's school performance, you may want to consider asking. If you aren't comfortable doing so, contact your school social worker, who can help.

▶ 3. Remember that parents of students with disabilities are important partners with you in the education of their child. Keeping them involved with their child's academic and behavioral progress throughout the school year can increase the possibility of success. Regular calls home, daily or weekly reports, or check-off forms are just a few ways you can help family members keep abreast of their child's academic and behavioral development. Also, some families may have e-mail addresses and are willing to share them with you. If this is the case, be aware that sending e-mail is not necessarily a private transaction. As a result, you may not feel comfortable sending sensitive information this way. If you do use e-mail, however, remember that any information sent via this method to parents must also be provided for those families who don't have a computer. Keep in mind that none of these communication methods is time-consuming, and each can win friends and influence people when you need parental support.

▶ 4. As a special education teacher, you will most likely be working with general education teachers who have your students in their class. You may want to talk with these teachers to decide who will be the one to contact families of the students with disabilities. It is often less confusing for everyone if only one teacher is the contact person, and usually the special education teacher works with the parents of students with disabilities. However, even though one teacher

Figure 8.1 Sample Introductory Letter to Parents of Students With a Disability

Dear parent or guardian,

We'd like to take this opportunity to introduce ourselves and to inform you of the special education program at our school. We are _____ (special education teacher) and _____ (general education teacher), and we will be team teaching in your child's classroom this year. Our inclusion program will provide your child with an opportunity to spend the majority of his or her school day working in the general education classes.

Our class is composed of students with a variety of strengths and educational needs. In an attempt to meet all the students' needs, we will be sharing teaching and classroom management responsibilities. Some of the behavior management strategies that might be used include daily reports, contracts, rewards, phone calls home, a classroom point system, and time out. Some teaching strategies we might use include team teaching, cooperative learning, and small group instruction. Additional behavioral supports and academic adaptations will be made as determined by the IEPs of students with a disability.

Please feel free to contact us at _____ if you have any questions or concerns. The best times to reach us are _____ or _____.

Sincerely,

Figure 8.2 Letter Sent to Parents of General Education Students

Dear parent or guardian,

We'd like to introduce ourselves and tell you a little bit about our classroom. We are _____ and _____, and we will be team teaching in your child's classroom this year.

Our class is composed of students with a variety of strengths and educational needs. In an attempt to meet all the students' needs, we will be sharing teaching and classroom management responsibilities. Some behavior management strategies we may use include rewards, phone calls home, a classroom point system, and daily reports. Some teaching strategies we may use include team teaching, cooperative learning, and small group instruction.

Please feel free to contact us if you have any questions or concerns at _____. The best times to reach us are _____ and _____

Sincerely,

may be the usual contact person, families should be made aware that other teachers are involved in the education of their child, and that they can communicate with any one of you when they desire to do so. When you do need to make a home contact, check with the other teachers to see if they have any concerns or perhaps positive information that they would like you to convey.

▶ 5. There will no doubt be times when you must contact family members due to academic or behavioral concerns. If you have done a good job of keeping lines of communication open, you will probably find them willing to work with you when problems arise. If they have never heard your voice except to blame or complain, your request for help may elicit a different reaction. Remember also that you will make parent conference and report card time much more comfortable for yourself, your students, and their parents if parents have been aware of an ongoing basis of any concerns you may have. There should be no real surprises at conference time (or in report cards). If there are continuing concerns, these meetings should provide time for a face-to-face discussion of how things are going and what more can be done, if necessary.

IEP Meetings

IEP meetings can be a daunting experience for some parents, so kindness and sensitivity on the part of all staff members should be the byword at these meetings. For some ideas on how you can make this a positive experience for families, read on. (Please note that IDEIA allows and encourages the use of alternative ways to hold IEP meetings such as conference calls and video conferencing. Be sure you know your school district's policy in this regard.)

▶ 1. This meeting can sometimes be difficult for families whether it is the initial placement meeting, an annual meeting, or a three-year reevaluation. Consider that when the family members come, they must face the fact that their child has been or might be diagnosed with problems that will affect or are affecting their performance at school and other areas of their life. This can be unsettling for the most optimistic of parents. As the special education teacher and the person who probably has the most contact with family members, consider it your job to help them feel comfortable. Be sure someone in the office knows they are coming and provides them with a place to wait if they are early. Greet them and if possible, take a little time to answer any last-minute questions. Be sure they are clear about which other professionals will attend the meeting and why they are there. It would be a nice gesture on your part if you contacted parents before the IEP meeting to find out if there are any special concerns they may want addressed. This phone call can also serve as a friendly reminder of the upcoming meeting.

▶ 2. Also, be aware that some families may feel intimidated by the group of professionals who may attend the meeting. Most support staff members have had experience working with parents and do their best to make them feel comfortable and welcome. But don't hesitate to question or clarify remarks or statements they make if you think parents may not understand or be confused—sometimes while talking, educators slip into jargon that family members may not understand.

If you think this might be the case, find a sensitive way to rephrase the remark or to ask the person who made it to do so.

▶ 3. In addition to avoiding the use of educational jargon, choose the words carefully to describe the student. Be sensitive to the connotations behind certain words. For instance, rather than describing the student as a sloppy worker, you could say, "needs to be more organized," or rather than labeling the student as a thief, describe his or her behavior in less inflammatory language by saying "takes things without permission." Also, show sensitivity when talking about the student's present level of academic performance. Unless required by your school district, consider providing descriptive information about specific academic tasks the student can and cannot do rather than providing grade-level equivalents. Imagine how devastating it could be for a family member, and especially the student, to hear that his or her reading level is significantly below grade level.

▶ 4. The IDEIA legislation has emphasized parental involvement in the IEP process. The IEP should be developed at the meeting and should not be brought as a completed document. One reason is to allow family members to have input, and sometimes we as professionals forget this. This is probably one of the most important things for team members to keep in mind throughout the meeting. As the special education teacher, take the responsibility to be sure parents—and students—have their say as the IEP is developed. Assuming parents have nothing to offer is assuming they know nothing about their own child.

▶ 5. Take the time to listen to parents. Hopefully, if the team has done its job well, family members will relax and become comfortable enough to share their concerns and other things that could prove very valuable to you in dealing with their child in the classroom. This might also be a time when you can have a productive discussion about classroom or behavior concerns. The results of these discussions can then be incorporated into the IEP, and the document will become what it was meant to be—a truly individualized education program for the student.

Parent Conferences

Conference time can be a golden opportunity for you as a special education teacher if you do some thoughtful planning. Many parents whom you might never see otherwise may make an effort to attend. It can be your one chance to encourage a good working relationship, discuss an issue face to face, or to reassure a concerned parent. Collaborating with your general education partners is a must to be able to present the whole picture to family members. Read on to see how you can make the most of this opportunity.

▶ 1. Unless you are in a self-contained classroom (where students with disabilities spend most of their school day), you will want to meet with the general education teachers to plan conference time. This planning, however, should not begin the week before conferences are scheduled. Early in the school year, you and the general education teachers should decide on such important issues as academic grading, collection of work samples, and documentation of social growth and behavioral issues for the students with disabilities. If this is done well in advance, then planning later in the year for parent conferences should go smoothly.

▶   2.   As noted above, thoughtful planning is a must. Each student is an individual, and each conference should reflect that. You might want to develop a form for your own use or even to give to the parents at the conclusion of the meeting. It could include such things as a brief comment on progress in academic areas that describes both a strength and an area of need and a comment on behavior and social interaction. In addition, one or two suggestions about how the family could help at home with specific skills the student is working on would be helpful. Of course, you will expand on each of these areas during the conference. This form can also serve as a way for you and your general education partners to plan. If you make this form something parents can take home, then they have a written record of what transpired. Most school systems encourage—and some even require—teachers to gather a compilation of student work that illustrates progress—or lack thereof. This will provide you with evidence to support what you tell parents about how their child is doing academically. Let parents take this work home to share and talk about with their child.

▶   3.   Parent conference time can also be an opportunity to talk about other issues. Personal care concerns are best discussed face to face, and this would be a good time to do so. In addition to general educators, you might want to ask your school nurse, guidance counselor, or the social worker to sit in and help with this delicate subject. Conference time is also an appropriate time to discuss behavioral concerns. But remember that if some of these problems have been ongoing, conference time should not be the first time parents hear about them. It is unfair to spring potentially sensitive issues for the first time at conferences. This time should be used to discuss progress and to decide whether other courses of action are needed.

▶   4.   It's always a good idea to begin and end the conference with something positive, even if you are only able to begin by saying how glad you are to meet your student's parents and end by saying that you are so happy he or she is in school every day. Starting with a kind word can help family members to be at ease and to be more open to what you have to say. Closing with something nice might help soften any negative parts of the conference so they can leave with the feeling that you care and are working for the best interest of their child.

▶   5.   Most family members are understanding and willing to work with you to help their child succeed, even when problems occur. Occasionally, however, parents or guardians, for whatever reason, come to the meeting feeling angry, belligerent, or defensive or they may become so as the conference progresses. If you have any reason to think that your meeting with specific parents may not go well, plan ahead. Alert your administrator, and let him or her know of your concern and what time the particular conference is scheduled. Ask whether the administrator could stand by to make him- or herself available should you need help. You and your general education partners may also want to consider asking another person to attend, such as the school social worker or psychologist, who may know about the child and family. If these individuals are unavailable, ask another teacher—perhaps someone who has had the child in class in the past. If you are alone in a self-contained classroom, you may also want to ask another teacher, or even someone from your building's special education administration, to accompany you. In situations such as this, it is always a good idea to have a witness. If possible, let the family members know ahead of time that someone else will be at the conference, and if it is someone who has had previous dealings with the child and family, or has something to contribute, it will not seem unusual. And remember to keep calm. Don't raise your voice or argue. If the parent(s) seem very unreasonable and cannot talk rationally, call your principal. Then let the parent know that you think it's best not to continue the conversation until the principal has arrived. At this point, your administrator may want to take over the discussion or may invite the family member(s) to finish the conference in his or her office, with or without you. Be sure your principal understands your side of the issue beforehand so he or she can put things in proper perspective.

Documentation

Brain overload is an occupational hazard for all teachers but especially for special educators. This is one good reason to document your communications with parents. Another is the ability to provide evidence of your attempts to contact family members. Read on to see how documentation can be an invaluable teaching tool.

▶ 1. As you become familiar with your students, there might be some who will cause you special concern because of ongoing academic or behavioral problems. As a result, you may find that you must contact family members frequently. If this is the case, consider developing a way to briefly document your contacts and attempts to make contact. Doing this is especially important if you are unable to reach parents a majority of the time. However, remember not to limit your efforts to daytime hours only. Try evenings or in the morning also to be sure you are giving people a chance to answer when they are home. Just a word of caution—if you choose to make phone calls from home, keep in mind that the family you are contacting may have a caller identification device on their telephone. You may want to consider blocking your phone number to keep your personal information from being disclosed.

▶ 2. You can make up a simple phone log form yourself, or use the one provided in Figure 8.3. If you design one of your own, be sure it includes the student's name; name of the person whom you attempted to contact; time and date of attempted contact; and whether you left a message, the line was busy, there was no answer, or the phone was disconnected. Also include a brief comment if you did reach someone. These are all-important items should you later need a record of your attempts to reach a parent or family member.

▶ 3. If you are unable to make phone contact with family members, try using some sort of daily report or other form of communiqué that can go back and forth with the student between school and home. Whatever you decide to use, leave a space in which both you and the parent can jot notes to each other. Some students may balk at having to take home a daily note, so you may need to build in some sort of incentive or reward to encourage the student to take it home,

Figure 8.3 School-Family Telephone Log

Student_____

Parent_____

Home Phone_____ Work Phone_____

Day	Time	*Response	Comments

*Response List:

A. Spoke with parent   D. Spoke with relative   G. Phone disconnected

B. Busy signal   E. No adult at home   H. Family initiated call

C. No answer   F. Parent declined to speak

Other _____

_____

have it signed, and return it to you. You can further increase the likelihood of it making its way home and back by including a positive comment whenever possible. Keep the returned forms in a file folder as a means of documenting parental involvement as well a way to provide a record of conversations between you and family members. If you are concerned that a note might not be returned to school, consider making a copy before sending it home or using carbonless premade parent notes that can be purchased in many teaching supply stores.

▶ 4. Keep notes on all of your parent conferences as well. Either during or shortly following the meeting, jot a brief summary on what you and the parent discussed as well as any recommendations for remedying the issues. As a courtesy, ask the parent if he or she would like a copy of these notes. If problems continue, or if the parents feel they were not made aware of concerns, these notes help refresh everybody's memory.

Assistance From School Support Staff

Whether or not you have parental backing in dealing with students with behavioral or academic challenges, remember that you are not alone. Support staff members can work with you alone as well as with involved family members to find ways to address concerns. Don't hesitate to call on them. Read on to see how you can enlist their aid.

▶ 1. If you feel additional input would be helpful regarding concerns you have about certain students, don't hesitate to involve support staff. (See Chapter 9 for more information.) Parents should be aware of the additional services that are available to them and their child at your school. If you feel it is appropriate, provide information about the kinds of services offered by the guidance counselor, school psychologist, school social worker, and other support staff. Depending on what the policies in your school district allow, you may be able to meet informally with parents and certain support staff members and of course formally at an IEP review meeting to develop strategies to help the student. Even if parents are not involved for whatever reason, support staff should be available to assist you with concerns.

▶ 2. The makeup of a support staff often varies from school to school, so be sure you know who is in your building—and get their schedules so you know when they are there. This staff could include one or more social workers; guidance counselors; school psychologists; speech and language, occupational, and physical therapists; and medical professionals such as nurses. Your school could also have others. It's a good idea to introduce yourself to these people, and tell them about your position and your students. In this way, if and when you need their help, with either students or parents, you won't be a stranger.

▶ 3. Be sure to ask which services these professionals provide in your school. See Chapter 9 for some of the services these individuals might be able to offer. You can request that these staff members meet informally with you and the parents of certain students of concern to offer suggestions. Don't hesitate to contact them on behalf of your students.

▶ 4. Most districts have a procedure used by support staff for referring students for formal services. Following this process is vital. Doing otherwise may jeopardize the positive relationship you want to foster with the professionals who provide these services. You might also want advice from support staff members about how you can talk with parents regarding concerns they have that prompted you to begin a formal referral process.

▶ 5. As the school year progresses, you may find that despite your best efforts, you have a student or students whose behaviors are becoming more alarming. This might be a good time to consider consulting one or more support staff members. Be sure you have gathered enough evidence, including the varied reward and consequence systems you have used, parent contact and involvement, whole-school discipline procedures, and anything else you have tried. This will show that you have made a good-faith effort to deal with the problem yourself before asking for help from a support staff member. The support staff may decide that the student would benefit from their services or they may determine that a formal behavioral plan is necessary. If an IEP team meeting is required, the appropriate support staff members could be included as part of the team.

Working With
Support Staff

This chapter is full of good news for special education teachers, and it starts with the fact that you are not alone as you work with your students with disabilities. These students often present numerous challenges to their teachers, and other professionals in your school are there to help you meet these challenges. New teachers are sometimes unaware that they can call on these people for assistance. Hopefully, this chapter will help you identify these colleagues and the ways they can be helpful to your students—and you.

Chapter Outline

- The IEP and Support Staff Involvement
- Support From the Special Education Administrative Staff
- Support From the School Psychologist
- Support From the School Social Worker
- Support From the Guidance Counselor
- Support From Transition Service Providers
- Other Support Staff

The IEP and Support Staff Involvement

The Individualized Education Program (IEP) and its development are not the sole responsibility of the special education teacher. It is legally mandated that information come from a variety of sources including the general education teacher, parents, and when appropriate, any support staff working with the student. Read on to see how you can be sure to get input from these people. (The information about school support staff came from the Wisconsin Department of Public Instruction (http://dpi.wi.gov/) and from the Cooperative Educational Service Agency 7 (http://www.cesa7.k12.wi.us.))

▶ 1. As you look over the IEPs for your students, you may see that other staff members are providing services for them. These could include speech and language therapy, occupational therapy, physical therapy, psychological services, and others. These professionals will contribute their own goal pages to the IEP. Remember to remind them well in advance of IEP meetings in which they must be involved.

▶ 2. The good news here is that these support staff members can do more for you and your students than just show up at the IEP meetings—so don't be shy about asking for their help. The speech and language therapist may have some suggestions for you about things you can do in your classroom to extend what he or she is teaching. The physical and occupational therapists may identify activities you can do with your students that can help develop skills they are working on. The psychologist may have tips and strategies you can use to develop social skills or to improve behavior. Don't hesitate to take full advantage of the valuable assistance these professionals can give you on behalf of your students.

▶ 3. If you have IEPs that include goals for supplementary services, be sure you communicate on a regular basis with the staff members providing these services. Remember that the IEP should provide a complete picture of the student, and as the keeper of the IEP, you should have a basic understanding of all aspects of this document. As time is usually at a premium for everyone, regular face-to-face conversations may not be practical. Most staff members have their own phones with voice mailboxes or often e-mail that can be used as a vehicle for sharing information. When you come to the IEP meeting, as the special education teacher there should be no surprises for you. Remember that parents look to you as the coordinator of their child's educational program, and though you can't be an expert on everything, you should be able to provide them with basic information on most aspects of this document.

▶ 4. Remember also that the IEP should be developed at the IEP meeting. Although most special education teachers come with suggested goals and objectives, there should be opportunity throughout the meeting for all professionals—and the family members (and student) present—to provide input. It is important to consider all contributions. Other staff or family members may have a perspective that could cause you to change your mind about a goal or objective you have developed.

▶ 5. Support staff members are part of a team of professionals that you should be able to count on for assistance. If you feel reticent about approaching them, keep in mind that you are doing it on behalf of your students, not yourself. Note that if consultation time with any of support staff is indicated on the IEP, then it is required by law that you meet with them for the designated amount of time to discuss the student's progress.

Support From the Special Education Administrative Staff

These are the special education experts in your building or within your district who are the go-to people for the most accurate information and answers to your questions. Be sure you get to know them, and never hesitate to take advantage of their expertise, particularly when you have questions that may have legal implications.

▶   1. Titles vary based on school districts, but most have people who supervise special education staff and speak for the district regarding special education issues. These people often provide updates on district policies and monitor compliance to the law. Someone like this may spend time in your school or be available via phone or e-mail. Know who this person is, their availability, and contact information.

▶   2. Supervisors are often very busy, but don't hesitate to ask for their expert advice when needed. Other special education teachers or even your school administration may be able to help you with many of your questions. But as noted in the introduction to this strategy, if you feel your question or concern may have legal implications of some kind, be sure to contact the special education supervisor—better safe than sorry.

▶   3. If you have questions for the special education administrator that aren't urgent, consider jotting them on an index card or small notebook as you think of them. Then make an appointment to talk when that person is in your building, or if he or she has an interoffice mailbox in your school, put your concerns in the mailbox along with your phone or extension number. This gives these busy people some options for how they can respond.

Support From the School Psychologist

These professionals can be a gold mine of information and support for special education teachers. You may be pleasantly surprised at some of the services school psychologists can provide for your students. Get to know them, and ask for their valuable advice and suggestions.

▶   1. School psychologists have specialized training in both psychology and education. They understand how school systems work, the elements of effective teaching, and the components of successful learning. They work with families, teachers, and other school staff to ensure that students are able to take full advantage of their educational opportunities. These professionals are also involved in testing students who are referred for special education services.

▶ 2. The psychologist in your school may be full- or part-time. Be sure you know when he or she is there and how you can contact this person. This person can provide a variety of valuable services to you and your students, such as consulting with you and the parents of your students about learning and behavior and working with students to evaluate academic skills, socioemotional development, behavior, and eligibility for special education. This person can teach individual students, small groups, and even whole-class lessons about conflict resolution, anger management, social skills, and so on, and can often provide strategies for learning and behavior management. There may even be a goal page on an IEP of some of your students that relates to psychological services. Obviously this person can provide much more than just testing results at an IEP meeting.

▶ 3. You may have students for whom you have serious concerns regarding academics, behavior, or social development that you might feel ill equipped to handle alone. You should not think you are an unsuccessful teacher if you don't have all the answers for the serious problems of some of your students. In fact, it is your responsibility to seek help from a professional who has additional training and experience—and your school psychologist could fill that bill. This person can also be a liaison between school and home and even the doctor's office. Having the additional support of the psychologist can sometimes help parents realize the seriousness of your concern. Don't hesitate to become familiar with the services this person can offer you.

▶ 4. In addition to working directly with students and their families, your school psychologist can also help you interpret test results and documents from outside services as well as provide you with information on specific mental health diagnoses.

Support From the School Social Worker

You may or may not be aware of all the valuable services your school social workers can provide for teachers and students. These professionals have specialized training in crisis intervention and in working with families, two areas that can be of real concern for teachers. So here is another resource to assist you in areas in which you feel you may need help.

▶ 1. Your school social worker is an integral link between school, home, and your community. This person works in collaboration with school personnel as a bridge for communication in these areas. Sometimes a family situation is so delicate that it may be uncomfortable for you to handle it alone. In this case, your school social worker could be a good person to call on. He or she has special training in crisis intervention and can help you deal with family members in a sensitive and appropriate manner. The social worker can also help parents access services from agencies and community organizations that can be of assistance to them. This person can help families with paperwork, insurance concerns, and can even locate an interpreter if needed.

▶ 2. Another important service your school social worker can provide is help with early identification and prevention of problems in school, another area in which his or her training in crisis intervention is crucial. The social worker can work with students who exhibit signs of socioemotional, physical, or behavioral difficulties that are interfering with their school adjustment and achievement.

▶ 3. This professional is another resource in helping students, individually or in groups, to better understand themselves and others, improve relationships, build self-esteem, cope with stress, and develop self-discipline.

▶ 4. The social worker may also be a good person to call on to assist parents in preparing for an IEP meeting. Sometimes family members of students with disabilities are confused and worried that their child is in a special education setting for all or part of the school day. They may be concerned about the implications of an IEP and how it will affect their child's future. Your social worker may be able to collaborate with you to help alleviate some of these concerns. He or she may be willing to attend the IEP meeting to help the family members understand the proceedings.

▶ 5. Special education teachers sometimes find that they must deal with an array of serious student and family concerns. Remember that your school social worker can be a real ally when you must deal with sensitive student or family situations and will do home visits to speak to parents when an issue warrants. Take the time to talk with this person to find out more about the services he or she can provide for you and your students.

Support From the Guidance Counselor

Another invaluable member of the school support staff is the guidance counselor. Guidance or school counselors can offer a wealth of services to students with disabilities, such as assistance with academic achievement, personal growth and development, and planning for life beyond high school. Continue reading to find out how a school counselor can help guide your students down the path of success.

▶ 1. Guidance counselors not only help students plan for the future beyond high school, but they also lend support to students regarding social, behavioral, and personal problems at home or school. For instance, this person may offer preventive instruction on topics such as drug and alcohol awareness, provide corrective instruction such as conflict resolution, or address specific concerns such as domestic abuse or failing grades. Guidance counselors may work one-on-one with a student, lead small groups, or work with an entire class. In addition to working directly with students, guidance counselors often collaborate with other school-based support staff, teachers, school administrators, parents, and outside service providers such as medical professionals.

▶ 2. IDEIA requires that the IEP team address transition services for students with disabilities beginning no later than the student's 16th birthday. One aspect of transition that needs to be addressed is that of appropriate academic course work to help prepare the student for postsecondary life. As most guidance counselors are involved in developing student schedules, you may want to invite the school guidance counselor to the IEP meeting; this person's expertise can prove invaluable when identifying courses of study the student must take to reach his or her postsecondary goal.

▶ 3. One of the major roles of guidance counselor is to advise students on post-secondary goals and plans. This person often works with students to identify possible career choices by administering aptitude assessments, interviewing students, or using some other means of assessment. For students who plan to attend a postsecondary educational institute, the guidance counselor can assist the student, and often the parent, in researching admission requirements, financial aid options, and supports provided to students with disabilities. For students who plan to go directly to a job following high school, the guidance counselor may teach job-search skills, such as completing an application and interviewing for a position.

▶ 4. As students progress through middle and high school, they are often subject to more pressure than they were at the elementary level. For instance, secondary school-aged students often worry more about their grades and life beyond high school, become more concerned about self-image and fitting in, and may feel more pressured to engage in risky behavior. These pressures are often magnified for students with disabilities. Because of their training, guidance counselors are better equipped than special education teachers to work with students who succumb to pressure and demonstrate such behaviors as suicidal tendencies, drug or alcohol abuse, sexual activity, or other harmful or dangerous conduct. If you, a colleague, or a parent is concerned about the behavior of a particular student, talk with the guidance counselor right away. Depending on the student's behavior, this person may choose to meet with the student or to offer recommendations about addressing the concern.

Support From Transition Service Providers

The question "what do you want to do when you leave high school?" makes high school students anxious and also may frazzle the nerves of special education teachers who worry about whether they are providing enough help to their students in making this decision. Fear not, for help is within your reach. Read on to find out about others who share in the responsibility of preparing students for post–high school.

▶ 1. Usually, there is a state-level person responsible for secondary transition issues. Titles vary from state to state, but this person may hold the title of secondary transition coordinator or something similar. Typically, this person helps develop and disseminate state or district guidelines regarding transition issues and provides technical assistance to schools, parents, and districts regarding transition guidelines. This person may offer professional development opportunities on the topic of transition, send bulletins to the school, or place information on a Web site. You should be able to find out the name of this person as well as information about the specific transition guidelines for your state or district on your state department of public instruction Web site as well as your district Web site.

▶ 2. Many high schools have a transition specialist or similarly titled person to help prepare students for postsecondary life. This person is typically a high school teacher with a variety of responsibilities. For instance, a transition specialist typically gathers information about the student's interests and abilities through interviews and other assessment instruments such as an interest inventory. Then, based on the results, the transition specialist collaborates with community businesses to provide the student with on-the-job training. To further enhance the learning experience, the transition specialist visits the job sites and works with the student in learning the job skills and then assesses performance. Depending on your school, this person may be assigned to your school full- or part-time. Find out who this person is so you can collaborate on providing transition services and determining when and if he or she should be invited to the IEP meeting.

▶ 3. In addition to school district employees, other professionals may be invited to the student's IEP meeting to provide input or offer services to help the student transition toward postsecondary life. These professionals may include vocational rehabilitation representatives, county services, current or future employers, county case managers, and independent living coordinators. Most school districts have a set policy in place regarding how and when to invite outside agency representatives. However, be aware that there are often waiting lists and eligibility criteria for accessing adult services, so waiting until the last IEP meeting before the student graduates may be too late.

Other Support Staff

In addition to the support staff previously discussed, there may be others in your school to assist your students. These could include an occupational or physical therapist and a school nurse. There may be others in your building. As the special education teacher, you may have students being serviced by some of them. Remember that these people are also part of the team that is in place to help you if needed.

▶ 1. Occupational and physical therapists work on helping students improve fine and gross motor skills, respectively. They may do this in your classroom or in another place in your school. Keep in mind that the things they work on are directly related to the student's performance in school, so it's a good idea to be aware of the goals they have for them. For example, hand and finger dexterity are important for writing and printing, among other school-related activities. Talk with the occupational therapist about these skills or others that may be targeted for your student, and ask about ways you can help the student practice them in your classroom. Large muscle activities are usually the domain of the physical therapist. Again, talk with this person to find out how you might work on skills with your student in class. Remember that what these individuals do is directly related to the student's success in your class or group. Helping your student may ultimately enable him or her to be more successful with the topics and tasks you are teaching.

▶ 2. Remember that you can also use the occupational and physical therapist as resource people. You may have students who do not qualify for their services but who could benefit from tips these professionals could offer you. So get to know them, even if they are not serving any of your students with disabilities. Find out when they are in your building. Contact them via e-mail, phone, or a note in their mailbox to save their time and yours—and keep your questions brief and to the point. Make it easy for them to provide information for you.

▶ 3. The school nurse is becoming a more frequent fixture in schools, and some schools even have clinics that serve the surrounding community. We are sometimes faced with students who are poorly nourished, have chronic health problems, or may occasionally come to school when they are sick and should be home. All teachers should be sensitive to and aware of the physical health of their students as this can directly affect their performance in school. Below are some ways a school nurse may be able to help with your students.

    a. The school nurse can be a valuable resource for you in several ways, so introduce yourself, and be sure you know when that person is in your building. If you have serious concerns that the health needs of a student are not being met, and you are uncomfortable with approaching family members, call on your school nurse. This person can be a liaison between you and the family, and it is possible that family members will be more open to hearing about these concerns from him or her. Also, be sure to check your students' IEPs to determine whether nursing services are required due to existing health problems. Students who have diabetes, seizures, asthma, or other serious health issues may have nursing services written directly into their IEP, making it mandatory to meet with the nurse to address these issues. Often, there are formal medical plans written by the nurse outlining the procedures to follow in dealing with these medical problems. Include copies with the student's IEP and with the general education teacher if the student spends any time in his or her classroom.

    b. You may be able to use the school nurse as a resource in dealing with sensitive personal-care-related issues. If you are uncomfortable contacting family members in this regard, the nurse can be the liaison. Don't hesitate to find out about the valuable services this person can provide.

▶ 4. The speech and language pathologist in your school is a professional who specializes in speech and communication development and disorders. This person provides services for students who have difficulty with communication skills that hinder their performance in reading, writing, listening, or speaking. General education students as well as students with disabilities may need services from this person. You may find some speech and language goal pages in the IEPs of some of your students.

▶ 5. Depending on your school district, a diagnostic teacher or program support teacher may be another resource person. This person may have other titles in your school system. He or she may conduct observations of students and administer testing as part of the initial evaluation for a potential disability. Typically, this person has a thorough working knowledge of the IEP and is up-to-date on any district changes. If you have any questions or doubts about what you have written, don't hesitate to contact this person. Relying on your own knowledge or even that of other special education teachers if you are in doubt about something may not be the best course of action. Remember that this person may not work in your building so be sure you know his or her telephone number.

10

Working With Teacher Assistants

"**B**ut I never took a class on how to work with and direct another adult!" If that was your first thought when you were assigned a teacher assistant, take heart. (Please note that titles for persons assisting teachers in their classrooms may be different in your school district. They will be referred to as teacher assistants or assistants in this chapter.) Kindness, respect, and a willingness to work together will go a long way in making this partnership a success. But you must be organized and have a game plan as you think about how your assistant can work with you for maximum benefit to your students. Consider the strategies below as you think about your approach to working with a teacher assistant.

Chapter Outline

- Making a Schedule
- Communication
- Presenting a United Front
- Assigning Responsibilities
- Discussing Concerns

Making a Schedule

If you are one of the fortunate few who has a teacher assistant, you know you have a responsibility to gain the maximum benefit from this help. Developing a schedule is one way to assure this will happen.

► 1. It is important that you know your school system's expectations for the role of a teacher assistant. There may be some limitations regarding what noncertified personnel can do, or there may be union restrictions. Check with your administrator or your union representative before you decide how you will use your assistant.

► 2. Once you are clear on what your assistant can do with your students, you are ready to develop a schedule. It's critical that you involve this person in this task for several reasons. You want them to be invested in what they are doing and to feel they have opportunity for input. In addition, a mutually planned schedule will help ensure there is no misunderstanding surrounding your expectations for your assistant. Furthermore, as you devise a workable schedule for your assistant, consider your schedule as well as your students' needs and their schedules. Look for classes held during hours in which you are unavailable to provide services to students, and assign your teaching assistant to these classrooms.

► 3. Despite the fact that you have a schedule for your assistant, there may be times when your administrator will need that person for another purpose. Be sure the classroom can still function. In other words, have a backup plan. Think about how you can work around the situation and still provide appropriate academic lessons for your students. Create your backup plan as soon as you have your assistant's schedule developed. Failing to do so will surely leave you in distress when the inevitable happens.

► 4. As the year progresses, you should monitor how well your assistant's schedule is working. Again, asking for input from him or her may provide insight you don't have or suggestions that would be valuable. If you find your assistant is not self-directed or for whatever reason has difficulty following the schedule, be sure to address the issue. Ignoring this can cause a breakdown in your class structure and tension that could affect your students.

► 5. Remember to continue the expectation for your assistant throughout the school year to follow the schedule you have both planned. Together, your goal should be to provide the best possible learning environment for your students. You can set a good example for your teacher assistant by being consistent in following your own schedule daily.

Communication

Never thought of yourself as "The Great Communicator"? Being able to do so with your teacher assistant can be crucial to the success of your partnership. And the success of this partnership can be crucial to your students' success, which should be the ultimate goal for both of you.

► 1. Working to make sure your assistant is invested in the success of your students should be your main goal. Involve this person in student-centered activities, not just copying materials and doing errands. This means you need to make it clear that you are willing, as far as possible, to include this person in the planning and execution of your lessons. If your assistant will be regularly teaching a certain type of lesson, you may want to model for him or her to be sure your expectations are understood. Remember to compliment and recognize success and appropriate initiative on the part of your assistant. The regular use of the words "please" and "thank you" go a long way in building respect and also provide a good role model for your students.

▶ 2. Don't feel threatened or slighted if your students relate well to your assistant. You may find he or she can work successfully with someone you might find difficult—and you may truly value this person's success with that student. Communicate your appreciation of his or her ability to establish and maintain a good working relationship with the students.

▶ 3. If your teaching assistant is supporting students in other classes, you may need to be the conduit between the other teacher and your teaching assistant. Given that it's highly likely that the teaching assistant walks into these classrooms at the same time as the students do, there may not be much time for the teacher and this person to talk about plans for the day. Find time to meet with these other teachers for suggestions on how the teaching assistant can support the student(s) in their particular classroom, and pass this information on to your assistant. Also make sure that the teachers know what they can and cannot expect from the teaching assistant. Make them aware that the teaching assistant is in their classroom to support the students, not to assist the teacher by grading papers or escorting students to and from the bathroom.

▶ 4. Sad to say, sometimes despite your best efforts and intentions, there may be difficulties with your assistant. First of all, realize that you are not the only teacher to experience this. Just because you are placed in a room with someone does not necessarily mean things will work out perfectly. Your administrator will, of course, expect you to make every effort to deal with your concerns before he or she becomes involved. As you work to resolve your difficulties, you may want to document what you have tried and the conversations you have had with your assistant. Then, should you or someone else need this information, you won't have to depend on your memory.

▶ 5. Finally, remember that the primary reason you have an assistant is to provide help to your students—but be sure this person isn't doing too much. He or she should not be doing the work for your students, and you need to communicate that. Furthermore, to help them do their job, make sure that your assistant has some knowledge about and understanding of the students' Individualized Education Programs (IEPs). You might even consider providing this person with a copy of the IEP snapshots for the students.

Presenting a United Front

"A house divided against itself cannot stand," Abraham Lincoln once said. This applies to you and your assistant as you work with your students. Presenting a united front is very important because students will recognize and capitalize on obvious differences and tensions.

▶ 1. It is imperative that you and your assistant present a united front to your class or group. A dangerous precedent will be set if your students think they can play one of you against the other. The job of both you and your assistant is to provide an appropriate academic, social, and behavioral atmosphere for your students. This can best be done if you can agree to manage these three areas as a team.

▶ 2. One of the best ways to ensure that you and your assistant are united in your efforts to educate your students is to make this person feel like a contributing and productive member of your teaching team. In addition to including your assistant in your planning and teaching, your students should be expected to treat this person with the same respect and deference with which they treat you. This can only happen if you make it clear through your own actions and words.

▶ 3. Keep in mind that you and your assistant are not in a popularity contest. View your relationship as that of two people having different things to offer to both the teaching situation and the students. Make an effort to recognize and appreciate what your assistant brings to your classroom and to your students— and stop to recognize and appreciate what you contribute as well.

▶ 4. You and your assistant need to be united about many things as you work together, but none more so than behavior management. Of course, you will have a behavior management program for your class or group, and you need to make sure your assistant understands your procedures. Your students should know they won't be able to play one of you against the other, that when one of you makes a decision, they cannot go to the other for a different outcome.

▶ 5. If you become concerned that your assistant is not on the same page as you and seems unwilling to support your classroom procedures and rules, address the issue. But find a way do so without blaming. Consider reviewing the procedures and rules, and ask for input from this person. This is another way of helping him or her to feel invested in what you are trying to accomplish with your students. Don't ignore a situation like this because it will cause tension and discomfort—and your students will be aware of what is happening and might try to capitalize on the circumstances.

Assigning Responsibilities

Do you think of your assistant as the queen (or king) of the copying machine? If this is the sum total of your job description for this person, you aren't using this wonderful resource to its fullest. Rethink your views, and begin adding a new dimension to your classroom or teaching situation.

▶ 1. Don't ignore this very important part of working with an assistant. Assuming that he or she will know what to do or can anticipate your needs or those of your students might have unfortunate consequences. Before you sit down with your assistant to discuss responsibilities (yes, it's important to include this person in the planning process), be sure to have a clear idea of what you would like him or her to do. Job responsibilities will typically include working with students as well as clerical work for you.

▶ 2. Talk with your assistant about any particular areas of strength or interest he or she may have that could benefit your students. If these can be used in your classroom or with your group, be sure to do so. But remember, you are the teacher and in charge of your students' educational experiences. Ultimately it is your decision as to which responsibilities you will assign your assistant.

▶ 3. Once you have decided on the division of labor, it's also your responsibility to monitor the work your assistant does, especially with your students. Be sure you are clear and specific in your assignments for this person. As time goes on, you may find that your assistant is self-directed and knows what to do with minimal instruction from you. But even under these circumstances, you still need to be sure appropriate educational practices are being implemented.

▶ 4. If responsibilities include work outside the classroom—whether clerical work for you or helping your students—you need to be aware of time spent on these projects. Most people have a good work ethic and will be aware of their time-related responsibilities to your and your students. But if you find your assistant disappearing for long periods of unaccounted-for time, you may need to tighten up that person's schedule.

▶ 5. Remember that making good use of your teacher assistant can double the educational effectiveness in your classroom. This can be especially important when you are working with students with special education needs as they often require a good deal of individual attention. This reason alone should motivate any good teacher to be sure time spent with a teacher assistant is used to the maximum benefit for their students.

Discussing Concerns

Every relationship encounters a bump in the road now and then, including ones in a classroom. If you have worked to develop a respectful and cordial partnership with your assistant by implementing some of the strategies in this chapter, it may be easier to get things back on track. Here are some additional ideas to consider if you conclude it's time to address a concern.

▶ 1. A successful relationship with your teacher assistant means you will need to be able to communicate when things are not going well. It's always best to confront small issues before they become big ones and get out of hand. Find a way to discuss your concerns in a friendly way without blaming anyone. Come to a definite agreement on how you both will handle the situation in the future— don't be ambiguous about what will be done.

▶ 2. The most important thing to remember is to address an issue early on. Don't wait and hope it will go away. It's much easier to nip something in the bud than to let it become a long-term habit. If you take care of things right away, it may just take a few minutes of friendly conversation rather than a long, tense discussion that could end with hard feelings. Remember too that tension in your classroom or group can be detrimental to your students, who usually know when something is wrong.

▶ 3. Another important thing to remember is to organize your thoughts, and be sure you have some examples of the situation that is causing you concern. Also, think about how you will approach the issue. Don't blame or use words like always and never. Listen calmly to what the other person has to say. Ask for input and ideas on how you can both work to solve the problem.

▶ 4. If your assistant seems upset or angry or refuses to acknowledge at least part of the responsibility for your concern, you may want to get some help. First, try someone in the building whom you trust and can talk to—perhaps another teacher or support staff member. Someone else may have a different perspective or an idea you haven't thought of. Don't go to your administrator immediately because he or she will expect you to do everything possible to solve the problem yourself first.

▶ 5. If difficulties persist, remember that it may be helpful to document examples of your concerns as well as the things you have done to address them. You don't need a long narrative—just sequential notes so you don't have to rely only on your memory. If you have arrived at this point, it may be time to meet with your administrator. If you decide to do this, remember to present the facts without blaming and to indicate your concern for the welfare of your students. At this point, your administrator should take the lead in assisting you in solving the problem.

11

Working With Administration

Developing a successful relationship with your school administration is very important for you and for your students with disabilities. Some administrators have had a great deal of experience working with students with disabilities while others have had limited opportunity. Whatever the case, you are still the first and best advocate for your students and will want to have a positive relationship with administration for your students' sake as well as your own.

Chapter Outline

- Understanding Your Principal's View of Special Education in Your School
- Communicating With Your Principal
- Principal Observations and Evaluations
- Professional Development
- What Is a Professional Learning Community?

Understanding Your Principal's View of Special Education in Your School

Attitudes toward providing services to students with disabilities run the gamut from a willingness to do everything possible to provide quality education to the students to a considerably less than enthusiastic stance. And sad to say, some of the reasons for this attitude can be laid at the feet of the special education staff.

Make up your mind that your professionalism, positive perspective, and dedication to educating students will impress your principal and help to put a positive spin on special education for him or her.

▶ 1. If you are new in a school, it probably won't take you too long to get an idea about staff perception of special education. Often this opinion is filtered down from the principal to teachers and other staff members. If you feel there is resistance within your school for whatever reason, decide you will do your best to help change it. Below are some ways to begin making changes that will help send a positive message about your professional commitment.

    a. Stick to your schedule—don't make last-minute changes unless you have a very good reason.

    b. Keep the general education teachers up-to-date with important information about your students.

    c. Take an active role within the general education classes in which your students with disabilities are included. Find out which students without disabilities could benefit from your help, and devise a plan to assist them while you support your students.

    d. Collaborate with general educators regarding field trips. Work together to determine if it's best for you to go along or stay back at school with students not participating.

    e. Be sure your paperwork is accurate and up-to-date.

    f. Keep your administrator apprised of any serious concerns regarding your students.

    g. If you are working with students who have a Behavior Intervention Plan (BIP), make sure the appropriate administrative staff members are aware of their role in implementing it. Be sure to provide them with a copy of this document.

▶ 2. Most middle and high schools have a principal and at least one assistant principal. If this is the case in your school, each administrator may take on specific responsibilities, and you may work with one administrator more frequently than others. For instance, some schools designate an assistant principal to each grade level or may have one administrator who oversees all students with disabilities. It is your responsibility to find out with whom you will be working.

▶ 3. Special education has undergone many transformations over the years, and there may be principals who are unaware of the latest legal and philosophical changes. It's up to special education administration and staff to help get them up to speed. Most school districts are now including students with disabilities in the general education classroom to the greatest extent appropriate rather than assigning them to a special education classroom. Some principals might have difficulty making the shift in thinking from the old idea of self-contained special education classrooms to inclusive, general education classrooms. As you assess your school situation, find out your principal's philosophy regarding special education. If you believe students with disabilities are not receiving the appropriate special education services, ask to meet with your administration to voice your concerns. Don't use this meeting to complain, but rather come prepared with suggestions for how change can be enacted on the basis of a student-centered rationale.

▶ 4. If you are concerned about the philosophy of special education in your school and believe changes are needed, remember that you need to work along with and not against the principal and your colleagues to help make this happen. If you are a new teacher, the best thing you can do is to demonstrate the dedication you have to your students through your professionalism and commitment to your responsibilities. As you become a respected educator in the eyes of your principal and other staff members, your ability to advocate for and implement change will grow.

Communicating With Your Principal

New teachers—and sometimes even veteran educators—might feel uncomfortable or intimidated by administration. But working to keep lines of communication open with your administrator can help alleviate some of these feelings. Looking for a way to do this in a relatively stress-free manner? Think about some of the suggestions below.

▶ 1. Consider a newsletter. The main audience for this, of course, would be parents and family members. But slipping a copy in your principal's mailbox is one sure way of letting him or her know what's happening in your classroom and with your students. If you feel overwhelmed with responsibilities, think biweekly or monthly—it doesn't have to be a weekly effort. Include such things as special activities or projects, classroom or individual student accomplishments (with student permission), upcoming tests, field trips, and so on. You could even have a section written by students. All these items are positive indicators of your efforts and progress with your students—something your principal will be glad to know about. A newsletter not only helps parents and others stay on top of classroom events, but it also allows you to communicate with your administrator without even setting foot in his or her office. You will appreciate this if you feel somewhat uncomfortable with communicating with administration or if time to meet is limited.

▶ 2. Communicate with your administrator to keep him or her informed about any escalating behavior situations with your students. If despite your best efforts—including various rewards and consequences, parent contact, and consultation with support staff—you continue to have serious concerns about a student, tell your administrator. He or she will not want to get a call from an irate parent or have a serious behavior incident occur at school without being forewarned of this possibility. In addition, make a point to update your administrator regarding ongoing concerns. If problems continue, talk to administration about the next step. If the student's behavior has improved, a quick thank you in appreciation of their support will be welcome.

▶ 3. In addition to keeping your administrator in the loop regarding serious behavioral concerns, share some good news about students who are consistently doing well or who have made improvement in their behavior or academic performance. You might even consider inviting your administrator to stop by to see a special lesson or project involving your students. Your own open-door policy sends a positive message about what you are doing with them. These positive interactions could be an icebreaker for you and a way to begin to feel comfortable about approaching your administrator.

▶ 4. If you do your best to collaborate with colleagues, attend to concerns regarding your students in a positive and proactive manner, and execute your paperwork correctly and in a timely fashion, you send administration the message that you are an asset to the special education staff and the school as a whole. This is one of the most important messages you can communicate.

▶ 5. If you are able to implement some of these suggestions, you will probably feel more comfortable with your administrators. You may even be ready to approach administration with new ideas or changes that would have a positive effect on your students. But remember that unless your administrator has an open-door policy, you need to make an appointment to talk. Be courteous, and let him or her know what you want to discuss ahead of time, come with an agenda, and don't overstay your welcome—remember that both of you are busy.

Principal Observations and Evaluations

Observations and evaluations by administration can strike fear in the heart of the most seasoned teacher. There are some things you can do well before your administrator sets a date to visit your classroom that will help minimize the trepidation you feel. Read on for ideas to help calm your nerves.

▶ 1. Consider asking your administrator to observe you informally throughout the school year. Ask for feedback, and accept criticism graciously. Think through how you could implement his or her suggestions. Follow up with a brief update on how things are going. Let your administrator know how you have incorporated the suggestions into your teaching as well as the impact on learning or behavior. If things are not going as well as hoped, be honest and ask for advice on how you could remedy the situation. Regular feedback from administration can provide you with invaluable advice that will help you grow as a teacher and help you to become comfortable with being critiqued—which will certainly help during formal observation.

▶ 2. It goes without saying that you should strive to have your day-to-day teaching be of the highest quality. You should not be putting on a show of good teaching only on the day your administrator observes you. If you are in the habit of regularly making lesson plans, preparing thoroughly ahead of time, and evaluating what you have taught on the basis of your students' progress, then you should be ready to be observed.

▶ 3. You should be able to get a copy of the evaluation form ahead of time. Look it over and identify strengths and areas of need in your teaching. You can then begin to work on things that need improvement.

▶ 4. You may be asked to provide a copy of your lesson plan prior to the observation. If not, you may choose to do so as it will enable your administrator to see how your lessons are developed around each student's educational needs and Individualized Education Program (IEP) goals. Make sure your lesson plan provides sufficient information to allow your administrator to follow instructions and to provide insight into your rationale for particular instructional techniques. For instance, you may have a student who is allowed to sit in the back of the room facing away from the rest of the class because that student is distracted by noise and activity. Without having been made aware of this, your administrator might question why this student is isolated from the group. You may even consider including IEP snapshots for each student for additional information.

▶ 5. Following the observation, if you feel the need to discuss your evaluation with your principal, be sure to make an appointment to do so. If you disagree with something, do so professionally. Don't whine or make excuses. Usually, there is a place on the evaluation form where you can write your own comments. Do so in a professional way. If you have serious concerns about your evaluation that cannot be resolved by meeting with your administrator, you may have the option of seeking assistance from the teachers' union in your district. But this should be a last resort. It is in your very best interest to try to resolve disagreements of this kind at the school level if at all possible.

Professional Development

Special education teachers today have to contend with constant changes in their field. New ways to teach, new criteria for disabilities, changes in documentation—these are all ongoing issues that face special educators. Although keeping abreast of these changes can be a challenge, your principal will expect you to do so. Here are some ideas that can help.

▶ 1. Professional development can take place in your school, within your school district, and out of the district. Find out from your principal how information about these opportunities is disseminated in your school. Speak with your special education administrator to be sure you are on a list to receive notices of any workshops or in-services in your field—especially those dealing with changes in documentation or service delivery for your district.

▶ 2. Your school may be a Professional Learning Community (PLC)—ask your principal or fellow teachers. The major focus of a PLC is to ensure high levels of learning for all students. A second focus is on the continual learning of teachers. The culture of the PLC school developed by the staff and administration is one of collaboration rather than teacher isolation. For more information, see the following strategy section and DuFour (2004).

▶ 3. Professional development can be as close as another teacher's classroom in your building. Ask your principal if you can observe a colleague for curriculum or management ideas. Look for someone in your building who has a strength in an area where you feel you need help. If you're not sure, ask the principal or another teacher to recommend someone for you to observe. Meet with that person beforehand to discuss what you will see, and then find time after the observation to discuss and corroborate what you saw. In addition, curriculum meetings, special education policy and procedure meetings, grade level meetings, and collaborative support teams for students who have academic or behavior needs are all opportunities for teachers to work together to share knowledge, ideas, and skills.

▶ 4. Frequently, school districts offer in-services for all teachers and some specifically for special education teachers. They can address documentation, curriculum, classroom management, technology, and more. In addition to the knowledge you gain from these meetings, you can also benefit from connecting with other special educators in your district. Often, the in-service presenters can help you find information, materials, or even put you in touch with other teachers who are working in situations similar to yours. Conferences and in-services from outside the district can also be informative. Usually there is a cost for attending, and often it is substantial, so be sure you talk with your principal to see whether funds are available through your school before you register. You could incur a significant personal financial expense if you fail to do so.

▶ 5. When making a request to your principal to attend an in-service, conference, or workshop, be sure to ask well in advance so any needed preparations can be made. Arrangements for a substitute may be necessary, you might have to submit in writing a formal request to attend, and there may be other procedures before things are finalized. Check with your principal to see exactly what is needed. Failing to follow the correct procedure could spell disaster for you and cause consternation for your principal on in-service day.

What Is a Professional Learning Community?

Professional Learning Communities (PLCs) have recently gained acceptance as a reform tool for schools in many parts of the country. The basic assumption of a PLC is that a school exists not only to teach students but to ensure that they learn. The shift is from teaching to learning and to finding ways of identifying whether learning is happening for all students. PLCs must consider what students should be learning, how teachers will know whether students are learning, and what they will do if some students are having problems learning.

Two important issues for schools that become PLCs are to recognize when students are having difficulty learning and to develop specific ways to ensure they succeed in the future. Schools that are PLCs are required to identify these students quickly and to intervene immediately rather than rely on remediation. Identifying data should be based on formative or ongoing assessment rather than summative assessment such as state-mandated tests. These schools are also expected to make it mandatory for these students to spend extra time and to receive additional help until they master the target skills or concepts taken from the formative data.

Teachers in PLC schools are also obliged to collaborate to ensure student success. Collaboration, a key word for PLCs, is defined as educators working as teams to evaluate and improve their classroom practices. The success of PLCs is based on results. Teachers work together to determine the current level of student achievement, establish a goal to improve, and work toward that goal. Finally, they must be able to show periodic evidence of success. Schools that become PLCs are obligated to ensure that all students learn, and the success of this program depends on the commitment and persistence of the educators themselves.

12

Working Within Your School Community

"No man is an island" is a quote that rings especially true in a school setting. Gone are the days when teachers close their doors and teach in isolation. This is particularly true for special educators. To help create the best possible learning environment for students with disabilities, it's up to us as teachers to pave the way by becoming full partners in the school community, with our general education colleagues, and other staff members. Read on for some tips on how to make this all-important partnership happen.

Chapter Outline

- Becoming Part of the Team
- Teacher Buddies and Mentors
- To Socialize or Not to Socialize
- The Teachers' Room
- Ask for Help, Offer to Help
- Other Supports for New Teachers

Becoming Part of the Team

Becoming a respected part of a school staff is especially important for special education teachers. Often, for reasons made clear in this strategy, special education teachers need to make an extra effort. Here are some sure-fire suggestions that can help accomplish that very important goal.

▶ 1. Special education teachers are like the new kid on the block—it seems we have to work harder at proving ourselves before we belong. How can you do this while still maintaining your integrity? If you are new in a school, there are some things you can do to help ensure that you become a valued team member. One of the best ways is to avoid the gossip mill. Don't get involved in school rumors and idle talk. Avoid becoming known as someone who spreads things about colleagues or students—true or untrue. Find trusted friends, be a trusted friend.

▶ 2. Be a team player. Offer to join a committee or two. Once on the committee, volunteer for a job you feel capable of doing. Participate in at least some optional or volunteer school activities. Show up, and stay till the end. Smile—even if you don't feel like it. Don't complain about school activities, policies, and goings-on—you never know who may be listening.

▶ 3. Some teachers may feel that special educators "work with only a small group of kids," "don't have to prep five classes," or "have all that extra time to do those IEPs." Often as special educators, we need to prove our worth. Here are some great ways to do that. Follow your schedule every day. If you are expected to be in a classroom at a certain time, be there. If on the rare occasion you must cancel, inform the other teacher as soon as possible. Don't be a wall-flower in the general education classroom. Assist students without disabilities in addition to your students, be an effective disciplinarian with all students, offer to help with field trips, and so forth. In other words, establish yourself as a bona fide teacher, not a helper teacher. Be a force within your school. See to it that students other than your own respect you and listen to you. Support other teachers' decisions. Ignore those who are special-education bashers. Work hard—prove them wrong.

▶ 4. If you are working within an inclusive education setting, you will also need to forge a professional relationship with the general education teachers with whom you will be working. Find out where and when your teaching unit meets. Prior to the meeting, ask one of your colleagues for an overview of what is typically covered during these planning meetings. For instance, do teachers plan thematic units, brainstorm ideas regarding students with behavioral or academic challenges, or share resources? Ask if there will be time for general education teachers to provide you with a quick update on the performance of students with disabilities. Come prepared with a few specific questions you want to have answered during the meeting, but remember to be brief as the team has other things to discuss in addition to special education issues. If your team doesn't regularly meet, consider making a lunch date to touch base with your colleagues about the needs of the students with disabilities in their class. But avoid meeting for the entire lunch period. Set an agenda and stick to it—you all deserve to have a little downtime in your workday.

▶ 5. Special educators also often meet as a department. Mark these dates on your calendar as these meetings can provide you with a wealth of information and support. Common discussion topics for special education department meetings include brainstorming strategies for specific students, sharing resources, coordinating services, and receiving updates on policies and procedures.

Teacher Buddies and Mentors

If you had one wish as a teacher, what would it be? Many of us would say we'd like another experienced and empathetic educator to confide in, someone who would take time to help and never make light of any question, no matter how basic. If you do have a buddy teacher or mentor, read on for some ways to nurture the relationship. If someone like that isn't assigned to you, look below for suggestions on how to find that person yourself.

▶ 1. Some schools and school systems have a buddy teacher or mentor teacher in place for staff members who are new. (Some systems have full-time mentors, but many have experienced teachers who mentor as part of their teaching responsibilities.) If you are fortunate enough to have a mentor, here are a few hints to make sure your relationship with that person flourishes.

   a. Be the first to introduce yourself at a time when your buddy or mentor is not busy. Then see if you can set aside a time that is convenient (especially for them) when you can regularly meet to talk.

   b. Respect your colleague by coming to your meeting on time and with specific questions you have jotted down—and limit your discussion to school-related topics, and keep it short and to the point. Your buddy teacher may be a classroom teacher too and have responsibilities he or she needs to attend to before or after your meeting.

   c. Don't complain and gossip during your time to talk. Doing so could put this person—whom you hope to make your ally—in an awkward position.

   d. Give your buddy teacher feedback. Make use of his or her suggestions and ideas, and let the buddy teacher know what worked. Thank him or her for the input. Share something new you've discovered that you think might interest him or her.

   e. If there is something you can offer your buddy teacher, do so. Perhaps you could share materials such as project ideas, academic games, or other things you have purchased for your students. Be sure to look for small ways throughout the school year to show your appreciation for his or her kindness—a favorite candy bar, soda, or snack as an occasional surprise would be welcomed by most.

   f. Remember that this person is taking time out of his or her day to help you. Your willingness to be considerate, respectful, and appreciative could ultimately earn you a trusted friend.

▶ 2. If your school has no one in place to act as a buddy or mentor for new staff members, there are some things you can do to find one. Find out if your school has a special education department chair, and meet the other special education teachers in the building. You may be able to connect with the person who had your students last year. This would be a good starting point for information and help. If you are the only special education teacher in your school, you may want to connect with one of the general education teachers who works with some of your students. In addition, many school districts allow teachers time to visit and observe classes in other schools. Take advantage of this opportunity if it is offered—you might make a new friend.

▶ 3. Be honest with the teacher with whom you are trying to make a connection. Tell him or her you have questions and concerns and would like someone to act as a sounding board on a regular basis. Ask the person if he or she would be willing, but don't be angry or upset if he or she is unable to help you; some people, for whatever reason, are uncomfortable in a mentoring position. If you find a willing person, be sure to follow the suggestions in step 1 of this strategy to ensure your relationship stays in good order.

▶ 4. Often, new special education teachers need help and guidance with the heavy load of paperwork responsibilities. Some of this paperwork is composed of legal documents that could be used in court, so it is very important that it be done in compliance with district and state regulations and laws. If you have questions about how to complete these documents, be sure to seek out someone who can give you accurate information. Your mentor or buddy teacher may or may not be that person. If you are unsure if you are getting correct information, seek out advice from a special education administrative person in your building.

To Socialize or Not to Socialize

Socializing can have a number of connotations in a school setting—some of them not so positive. Sometimes it is equated with gossiping or spending too much time standing in the hall talking, oblivious to the student chaos around you. On the other hand, getting to know your fellow teachers in a friendly and appropriate way is important. Striking a balance is the trick.

▶ 1. As previously discussed, special education teachers sometimes need to prove their worth to other staff members, and often the way your colleagues view you is the way they view your students with special education needs. You may need to be the good-will ambassador—for both yourself and your students. The best way to do this is to build a positive reputation. Remember the suggestions provided in Chapter 11, Working With Administration? Look them over again; they bear repeating. These tips are sure-fire ways to gain support and respect from your colleagues as well.

▶ 2. Remember that you can be cordial and pleasant without being a social butterfly. Greet your colleagues with a kind word and a friendly smile—no matter how you are feeling. Respond to requests, questions, or concerns from other teachers in a gracious manner. Be a team player. Join a committee or two, or volunteer for something. Work to be viewed as a welcome addition to your school's staff because of your attitude as well as your professional skills.

▶ 3. As you establish yourself as a respected person in your school, you will become comfortable finding appropriate ways to socialize with others. Those teachers who have the same professional philosophy as you do will gravitate toward you and you will develop a circle of trusted friends. As you work in your school and observe its culture and dynamics, you will find out where you fit, and the group of teachers with whom you are comfortable. You will be able to make decisions as to how and where you spend you precious free time during the school day. Then you can decide for yourself what part socializing plays in your school day.

The Teachers' Room

An important place in every school, the teachers' room can be a place to escape for a few minutes of solace—to have a quiet lunch or just to take a deep breath. But it can also be a hotbed of gossip and complaints. It's up to you to decide if and when you want to spend time there. Consider some of the following as you make up your mind.

▶ 1. Inevitably, you will need to decide where you want to spend your lunchtime and those precious few free moments, and the teachers' room may seem the logical choice. Here are some things to think about as you make your way there. If you enjoy socializing, consider that the definition of this word in the teachers' room could be gossiping or griping. This could include grumbling about other staff members, the principal, a parent or student, or how things are done at your school. Avoid adding your own two cents—gossip travels quickly, and you will be amazed how fast other staff members will know about "what the new teacher said." If you decide to visit the teachers' room, observe and listen during your first few visits. Then decide what the definition of socializing is in your school and whether or not you want to be part of it.

▶ 2. If grumbling and complaining are a regular part of the dynamics of your teachers' room, you may want to find another place to go. This kind of dialogue can be disillusioning and distressing, especially for newcomers to a school. One of your goals as a new teacher should be to make up your own mind in an objective fashion about other teachers, your principal, the students, and parents. Give yourself time to do this before you listen to others' opinions.

▶ 3. All educators need time to themselves, and it is important that new teachers take some time to regroup during the school day. Usually, the lunch hour provides this opportunity. If the teachers' room doesn't work for you, consider staying in your own room, eating lunch with another teacher, taking a walk, or even buying lunch at a fast-food restaurant occasionally. Teaching can be very intense, so don't underestimate the need to get away—and remember that you have several options.

▶ 4. Sometimes the teachers' room gripe sessions extend out into the hallways and to groups of teachers who gather to gossip there. It's usually wise to avoid involvement. You will want to be identified by your principal and other teachers as someone who is professional and who takes their responsibilities seriously. Gabbing while students in the hall may need monitoring or while they are alone in the classroom doesn't create a good impression. And as a special education teacher, you are often under extra scrutiny. Some people still think you are not very busy because you work with a limited number of students.

Ask for Help, Offer to Help

To have a friend, you have to be one. This adage certainly applies to you as a special education teacher, and abiding by this saying can have some positive results for you. Look below to see how reaching out to colleagues can reap benefits for you, and your students.

▶ 1. If you are a new teacher, you probably have many questions and requests for your more experienced colleagues and wonder what you could possibly have to offer them. As a special education teacher, there are many ways you can repay your general education colleagues for their help. This kind of give-and-take is a very important way for you to gain credibility and good will in your school—something that can benefit both you and your students.

▶ 2. During the first few weeks of school, you will probably be able to identify those people in your school who are friendly and willing to help. Most teachers who extend a helping hand do so because they remember what it was like to be new and to feel alone. Don't hesitate to approach them, but when you do so remember your manners. Arrange to meet at a time convenient for or them, get to the point, and say thank you.

▶ 3. At some point, you may feel you would like to reciprocate their kindness. Here are some ideas to consider.
   a. Share some useful teaching "how to" books, project ideas, or academic games.
   b. Use your own expertise as a special education teacher. Offer to include one or more students from the general education classroom in your groups if there are some who could benefit.
   c. Provide academic and behavioral adaptation ideas that may be helpful for some of the aforementioned students. But do so in a sensitive way. Don't assume your colleague is unable to adapt work or has never done so.
   d. Make an effort to assist on field trips for classes in which your students with disabilities are included. You might need to change your schedule, but your efforts to be part of the team will be appreciated. If you teach in a more restrictive setting, ask if your students can be included if you and an adequate number of assistants accompany them.
   e. Share materials, offer to substitute for a duty, or buy your colleague his or her favorite candy bar, soda, or snack.

▶ 4. You'll be surprised at the good will you can create and the respect you will gain for yourself if you accept kindness from others, and repay them. An added benefit is that your students will gain also. Teachers who respect you as a professional may be more willing to work with your students, and this is perhaps the best outcome of your efforts.

Other Supports for New Teachers

Most districts have avenues of support for new teachers outside of their schools. Find out what they are, and take advantage of them. These may differ slightly from district to district, but they are there. So be sure to find out what your school system has to offer.

▶ 1. Your district should have workshops and other educational opportunities to offer—and sometimes these are free. There are usually a number of topics for special education teachers, but don't hesitate to attend workshops that may be earmarked for regular education teachers such as those dealing with curriculum development in specific subject areas. Your goal, after all, should be to see that your students are able to access the general education curriculum as much as possible. It's therefore your job to be up-to-date on the latest subject matter and methods of teaching. Buddy teachers, other special education teachers, your administrator, or the special education supervisor should be able to help you access these opportunities.

▶ 2. Most school districts have teachers' unions that can help you if you feel problems in your school situation are not being addressed by your administration. Within your school, there will most likely be a union representative who may be able to answer some questions for you or direct you to someone in the union who can be of assistance. Certainly use these resources if you feel it necessary, but do make every effort to work with those within your school to address your problem(s) first. Most people outside your school to whom you go for help will want to know what you have done to address the problem within the chain of command in your school.

▶ 3. As a special education teacher, you should have a special education department in your district with a support staff available to you. This department may offer workshops or in-services also. Find out how you can get on their mailing list so you know about offerings that may be of interest. In addition to workshops, the support staff may be available to come out to your school to discuss concerns about your students or suggest academic and behavioral strategies that you could use.

▶ 4. There may be a technology department in your district that includes assistive technology for students with special education needs. This department might also offer in-services or workshops and may have a variety of things they loan out to teachers. Be sure you know how to access this in your district so that you know what is available.

■ References

Boynton, M., & Boynton, C. (2005). *The educator's guide to preventing and solving discipline problems.* Alexandria, VA: Association for Supervision and Curriculum Development.

Dieker, L. (2001). What are the characteristics of effective middle and high school co-taught teams for students with disabilities? *Preventing School Failure, 46*(1), 14–23.

Dieker, L. (2002). *Co-teaching lesson plan book: Academic year version.* Port Chester, NY: National Professional Resources.

DuFour, R. (2004). What is a professional learning community? *Educational Leadership, 61*(8), 6–11.

Friend, M., & Bursuck, W. (2002). *Including students with special needs.* Needham Heights, MA: Allyn & Bacon.

Friend, M., & Bursuck, W. (2006). *Including students with special needs.* Needham Heights, MA: Allyn & Bacon.

Friend, M., & Cook, L. (2003). *Interactions: Collaboration skills for school professionals* (4th ed.). New York: Longman.

Lindberg, J., Evans Kelley, D., & Swick, A. (2005). *Common-sense classroom management for middle and high school teachers.* Thousand Oaks, CA: Corwin Press.

Spinelli, J. (1990). *Maniac McGee.* Boston: Little, Brown and Company.

Tomlinson, C. (1999). *The differentiated classroom: Responding to the needs of all learners.* Alexandria, VA: Association for Supervision and Curriculum Development.

Vasa, S. F. (1981). Alternative procedures for grading handicapped students in the secondary schools. *Educational Unlimited, 3*(1), 16–23.

Walsh, J., & Jones, B. (2004). New models of cooperative learning. *Teaching Exceptional Children, 36*(5), 14–20.

Ysseldyke, J. E., Algozzine, B., & Thurlow, M. L. (2000). *Critical issues in special education* (3rd ed.). Boston: Houghton Mifflin.

Web Sites

Capstone Press: www.capstonepress.com

Center for Applied Special Technology: http://cast.org/pd/tes/index.html

Center for Effective Collaboration and Practice: http://cecp.air.org/fba/default.asp (see Parts 1 and 2)

Cooperative Educational Service Agency 7: www.cesa7.k12.wi.us

Creative Presentation Resources, Inc.: www.presentationresources.net (search "instant whiteboard")

Don Johnston: www.donjohnston.com

Families and Advocates Partnership for Education (FAPE): www.fape.org

Functional Behavioral Assessments and Positive Interventions: What Parents Need to Know: www.pacer.org/parent/php/PHP-c79.pdf

Intervention Central: www.jimwrightonline.com/php/jackpot/jackpot.php

IDEA 2004 Close Up: Transition Planning: www.schwablearning.org/articles.asp?r=998&f=search

Learning Toolbox: http://coe.jmu.edu/LearningToolbox/index.html

National Association of School Psychologists: www.nasponline.org/advocacy/ideainformation.aspx

National Center for Learning Disabilities: www.ncld.org

National Center on Secondary Education and Transition: www.ncset.org

Online Academy: www.onlineacademy.org/acad/products/contentpbs.html

Perfection Learning: www.perfectionlearning.com

Power of 2: www.powerof2.org

Roadmap to IEPs and IEP Meetings: http://www.wrightslaw.com/idea/art/iep.roadmap.htm

Schwab Learning: A Parents Guide for Helping Kids with Learning Difficulties: www.schwablearning.org

State of Wisconsin Department of Public Instruction: http://dpi.wi.gov/sped/sbiep.html

Update on IDEA 2004 Regulations (05/02/06): http://www.wrightslaw.com/news/06/idea.regs.0502.htm

Wieser Educational: www.wieser-ed.com

Wrightslaw: www.wrightslaw.com

■ Suggested Readings

Boynton, M., & Boynton, C. (2005). *The educator's guide to preventing and solving discipline problems.* Alexandria, VA: Association for Supervision and Curriculum Development.
This book provides strategies and recommendations for addressing discipline problems at the building level and classroom level, as well for working with challenging individuals.

Jensen, W. R., Rhode, G., & Reavis, H. (1994). *The tough kid toolbox.* Longmont, CO: Sopris West.
This book supplements *The Tough Kid Book* with more in additional strategies and more in depth explanations. Most helpful are the many reproducibles that accompany the strategies included here as well as those found in *The Tough Kid Book.*

Johns, B., & Carr, V. (2002). *Techniques for managing verbally and physically aggressive students* (2nd ed.). Denver, CO: Love.
This book has dozens of new strategies for working with violence and behavior in our schools. The authors provide how-to information and step-by-step methods for working with disciplinary problems and aggression within the school setting.

Johns, B., Crowley, E., & Guetzloe, E. (2002). *Effective curriculum for students with emotional and behavioral disorders.* Denver CO: Love.
This book explains how to create specialized instruction based on the individualized needs of students with emotional and behavioral disorders and demonstrates throughout how to plan a curriculum based on a diagnostic prescriptive approach.

Kottler, J. (2002). *Students who drive you crazy. Succeeding with resistant, unmotivated, and otherwise difficult young people.* Thousand Oaks, CA: Corwin Press.
This inspirational handbook offers the tools necessary to combat frustrating, hostile interactions, so you can remain motivated, effective, and successful when working with students who challenge you.

Lindberg, J., Evans Kelley, D. & Swick, A. (2005). *Common-sense classroom management for middle and high school teachers.* Thousand Oaks, CA: Corwin.
This book covers more than 65 best practices for managing the typical school day such as creating a positive classroom atmosphere, working with diverse student and family populations, and dealing with challenging students and situations.

Mannix, D. (1998). *Social skills activities for secondary students with special needs.* San Francisco, CA: Jossey Bass.
This book contains 187 ready-to-use worksheets to help students in grades 6–12 build the social skills they need to interact effectively with others and to learn how to apply these skills to various real-life settings, situations and problems.

McEwan, E. K. (2005). *How to deal with parents who are angry, troubled, afraid, or just plain crazy.* Thousand Oaks, CA: Corwin Press.

Every educator will find invaluable strategies for handling angry and unresponsive parents and the critical issues that cause misunderstandings.

Mendler, A. (1997). *Power struggles: Successful techniques for educators.* Rochester, NY: Discipline Associates.

This quick-and-easy-to-read book offers proven, practical strategies for preventing power struggles between educators and students.

Orange, C. (2000). *25 biggest mistakes teachers make and how to avoid them.* Thousand Oaks, CA: Corwin Press.

This book offers insight about how to be a more sensitive and effective teacher by analyzing the mistakes of other teachers. Learn how to avoid the most common and hurtful mistakes so that students can be more successful learners.

Orange, C. (2005). *44 smart strategies for avoiding classroom mistakes.* Thousand Oaks, CA: Corwin Press.

This dynamic, hands-on text presents finely honed strategies for creating flexible lesson plans and maintaining enjoyable classrooms that run like well-oiled machines. Also included are tips for motivating students, managing paperwork effectively, and much more to help teachers create an environment that is conducive to better teaching and learning.

Rhode, G., Jenson, W., & Reavis, H. (1992). *The tough kid book.* Longmont, CO: Sopris West.

This very practical book bypasses idealistic suggestions for dealing with difficult students and offers insight into a variety of inappropriate student behaviors. It provides a variety of workable and effective strategies to try that are useful at all grade levels. Many reproducibles are included.

Salend, S J. (2001). *Creating inclusive classrooms: Effective and reflective practices* (Rev. 4th ed.). Upper Saddle River, NJ: Prentice Hall.

This very thorough book covers a broad range of special education subjects including understanding the diverse educational needs of students with disabilities, differentiating instruction in academic areas, creating collaborative relationships, and fostering communication. Useful web sites are listed throughout, and a compact disc titled "Developing Quality IEPs: A Case-Base Tutorial" is included.

Sprick, R., Garrison, M., & Howard, L. (1998). *CHAMPS.* Longmont, CO: Sopris West.

Many useful proactive and positive approaches to classroom management and for dealing with a variety of inappropriate behaviors can be found in this book. Some reproducibles are included.

Tomlinson, C., & McTighe, J. (2006). *Integrating differentiated instruction and understanding by design.* Association for Supervision and Curriculum Development, Alexandria, VA.

This book examines the essential underpinnings of both Universal Design and Understanding by Design and demonstrates how the logic of each intersects with the other to promote classrooms that provide rich, durable, meaningful curriculum for the full range of learners that populate today's schools.

Vitto, J. (2003). *Relationship-driven classroom management. Strategies that promote student motivation.* Thousand Oaks, CA: Corwin Press.

This book combines resiliency, classroom management, and discipline into one user-friendly format suitable for all teachers. It features case examples, questions, classroom strategies and tips, and chapter objectives and summaries. The chapter material covers both Preventive Strategies and Reactive Strategies.

■ Index